P9-DEB-785

*Why Didn't
I Say <u>That</u>?!*

Why Didn't I Say That?!

What to Say And How to Say It in Tough Situations on the Job

Donald H. Weiss

American Management Association
New York • Atlanta • Boston • Chicago • Kansas City • San Francisco • Washington, D.C.
Brussels • Mexico City • Tokyo • Toronto

Library of Congress Cataloging-in-Publication Data

Weiss, Donald H., 1936–
        Why didn't I say that?! : what to say and how to say it in tough
situations on the job / Donald H. Weiss.
            p.   cm.
    Includes index.
    ISBN 0-8144-0209-7
    1. Communication in personnel management.   2. Interpersonal
communication.   I. Title.
HF5549.5.C6W448   1994
650.13—dc20   94-18556
                                                                    CIP

Printing number

10   9   8   7   6   5   4

Contents

Introduction   1

    Why a Book of Scripts?   1
    Who Should Read This Book   2
    How You Should Read This Book   2

SECTION I
Fundamentals of Managing Discussions: Communicating,
Giving Feedback, Problem Solving, and Encouraging   5

Chapter 1:   Four Basic Steps to Effective
Communication   7

    Dialogs
    Disagreeing with the Boss—The Ideal
      Situation   8
    Disagreeing with the Boss—The Exchange   9
    Disagreeing with the Boss—Resolving
      Differences   12
    Disagreeing with the Boss—Action
      Planning   14
    Conclusion   15

Chapter 2:   Giving Feedback   16

    Dialogs
    Positioning Feedback—The Ideal Situation   16

Positioning Feedback—Defensive
    Employee   18
Conclusion   22

Chapter 3: Problem Solving   **23**

Dialogs
Identifying Problems—The Ideal Situation   24
Identifying Problems—Uncooperative
    Employee, Part 1   25
Solving Problems—Uncooperative
    Employee, Part 2   28
Solving Problems—Uncooperative
    Employee, Part 3   30
Solving Problems—Uncooperative
    Employee, Part 4   31
Solving Problems—Uncooperative
    Employee, Part 5   32
Solving Problems—Uncooperative
    Employee, Part 6   33
Conclusion   34

Chapter 4: Encouraging Others   **35**

Dialogs
Encouraging a Withdrawn Person to Open
    Up—The Ideal Situation   36
Encouraging a Withdrawn Person to Open
    Up—Difficult Situation, Part 1   38
Encouraging a Withdrawn Person to Open
    Up—Difficult Situation, Part 2   40
Encouraging a Withdrawn Person to Open
    Up—Difficult Situation, Part 3   43
Conclusion   44

SECTION II
Interviewing Prospective Employees and
New Employee Orientation   47

Chapter 5: Interviewing Prospective Employees   **49**

Dialogs
Interviewing for a New
    Employee—Qualified But Shy Applicant   50
Interviewing for a New Employee—A
    Perfect Fit, Part 1   53
Interviewing for a New Employee—A
    Perfect Fit, Part 2   56
Interviewing for a New
    Supervisor—Reasons for Rejection   60
Interviewing for a New Supervisor—Hiring
    the Right Supervisor   61
Conclusion   65

Chapter 6: Providing Effective Orientation   **66**

Dialogs
Creating a Psychological
    Contract—Reassuring a New Employee   67
Creating a Psychological
    Contract—Orientation for an Employee
    without Job Experience   69
Conclusion   73

SECTION III
Performance Management: Reviews,
    Appraisals, and Coaching   75

Chapter 7: Reviews and Appraisals   **77**

Dialogs
Informal Review with Positive
    Feedback—The Ideal Situation   78
Informal Review with Negative
    Feedback—Reviewing Poor Performance   80
Collaborating on Writing a Performance
    Appraisal—The Ideal Situation   83
Collaborating on Writing a Performance
    Appraisal—Surly Employee   85
Conclusion   89

Chapter 8: Coaching to Improve Performance **90**

Dialogs
Missing the Mark—The Ideal Situation 91
Missing the Mark—Defensive Employee 95
Conclusion 99

Chapter 9: Coaching for Growth and Development **100**

Dialogs
Coaching a Reluctant Employee 101
Getting to Know Your Employees—The
  Ideal Situation, Part 1 105
Getting to Know Your Employees—The
  Ideal Situation, Part 2 109
Conclusion 110

SECTION IV
Managing Relationships 113

Chapter 10: Communicating with Difficult People **115**

Dialogs
Communicating with Someone Who
  Claims to Know Everything 116
Communicating with Someone Who
  Doesn't Speak Up 120
Conclusion 123

Chapter 11: Managing Differences **124**

Dialogs
Managing Differences of Beliefs and
  Values—Talking with a Judgmental
  Person 124
Confronting a Potentially Hostile
  Situation—The Ideal Situation 129
Managing Deliberate Discrimination or

Harassment—Talking with a Close-
Minded Person   131
Confronting a Man Sexually Harassing a
Woman—Stopping a Hostile
Environment   133
Conclusion   136

Chapter 12: Investigating Harassment Claims   **137**

Dialogs
Investigating a Charge of Sexual
Harassment—Angry Woman   137
Investigating a Charge of Sexual
Harassment—Defensive Alleged
Harasser   144
Investigating a Charge of Sexual
Harassment—Reluctant Witness   149
Conclusion   152

Chapter 13: Building Relationships   **153**

Dialogs
Building a Relationship with an Employee
Suspicious of Your Motives   153
Building a Relationship with a Competitive
Peer   157
Building a Relationship with Your Boss—A
Boss Everyone Else Resents   160
Conclusion   162

SECTION V
Disciplining, Firing, and Implementing a
Downsizing Decision   163

Chapter 14: Taking Corrective Action: Performance
Probation and Dismissal   **165**

Dialogs
Taking Corrective Action—Oral
  Warning—The Ideal Situation   166
Taking Corrective Action—Oral
  Warning—Angry Employee, Part 1   169
Taking Corrective Action—Written
  Warning—Angry Employee, Part 2   171
Taking Corrective Action—Dismissing an
  Employee—Angry Employee, Part 3   176
Conclusion   177

Chapter 15: Firing Rule Breakers   **178**

Dialogs
Communicating the Rules—The Ideal
  Situation   178
Counseling in Relation to the
  Rules—Rebellious Employee, Part 1   180
Warnings of Corrective Action—Rebellious
  Employee, Part 2   182
Dismissing an Employee for Disciplinary
  Reasons—Rebellious (and, Now, Angry)
  Employee, Part 3   185
Conclusion   187

Chapter 16: Implementing the Decision to Downsize   **189**

Dialogs
Laying Off Valuable Employees—Telling an
  Employee She Is Being Let Go   191
Laying Off Valuable Employees—Listening
  to an Angry Employee   193
Helping the Survivors—Enlisting the Help
  of an Angry Survivor   195
Conclusion   198

EPILOGUE
Some Final Words about Management Style   201

Index   205

Introduction

How many times, long after the fact, have you slapped your forehead with the palm of your hand and moaned, "I should've said—" or "Why didn't I say—"? Now, with this book, you may just say the right thing at the right time.

Why a Book of Scripts?

Most people handle themselves fairly well in ordinary, everyday conversations. But conversations can be anything but ordinary, and when they are, you may be at a loss for words just when you need them the most. Given today's stresses, even the great Greek orator and lawgiver, Solon, might find himself fumbling for the right thing to say, at the right time, in the right way.

This book consists of *suggestions*—models or simulations, not prescriptions—for ways of talking with people in business situa- tions that perhaps you haven't considered. Some of those situations can be somewhat sticky, as when you tell an employee that he is performing below standard. Read and practice these scripts and adapt them to your personal style or to your situation, but *don't* memorize them.

Actors make it all seem so easy. "Frankly, my dear, I don't give a damn." "Really, dahling. How could you?" "Play it, Sam. You played it for her. Now, play it for me." Famous words, said in their famous way. But those legends of the cinema had scripts from which they read their lines, and they had many rehearsals and takes. We ordinary mortals should have it so good.

This book of dialogs may not immortalize your conversations, but it will make difficult situations a little easier. When you are

confronted with a difficult person, an employee who isn't performing up to standard, or a boss who demands too much, review some
relevant scripts. They will help you plan how to cope effectively
with the situation and guide the conversation into productive out-
comes for everyone.

*However, planning in advance for a specific conversation isn't al-
ways possible.* "Hold it, boss; let me look up a snappy comeback in
my book of scripts" won't work. Therefore, the planning I'm refer-
ring to is often playing a game of "what if": "What if the person I
have to do business with is rude and inconsiderate? How would I
manage that?" This sort of mental exercise as you read the scripts
allows you to rehearse and prepare for the possibilities.

On the other hand, *planning in advance for a specific conversation
is sometimes possible.* When time permits—as when you have a
scheduled meeting with your boss or an underachieving employee—a quick reading of some relevant scripts (and a rehearsal,
if possible) will put you into a frame of mind that allows you to
engage in constructive discussion or dialog.

I'm also assuming that when your needs or rights or job requirements are at stake, you're willing to take control of the conversation. That doesn't mean overpowering the other person.
Rather, it means guiding the discussion or dialog toward a mutually beneficial outcome. *Proactive, positive stance, problem solving, decision making, encouraging, supporting, guiding, meeting needs,
fulfilling goals, satisfying values:* these are the words that characterize
the approaches of these scripts.

Who Should Read This Book

If you manage people or work closely with peers or people in other
departments, take this book to heart. If you're a spouse, a significant other, or a parent, you can use the guidelines that these scripts
provide and adapt them to your personal needs. Managing is managing, whether in your business life or your personal life.

How You Should Read This Book

Read this book with an eye toward becoming a more effective com-
municator, a more productive supervisor, with whom other people

want to work and with whom they enjoy talking. This is a lofty goal, perhaps, but not out of reach.

The chapters in Section I, "Fundamentals of Managing Discussions," provide the foundation on which almost all of the scripts are built. The skills they emphasize—managing a discussion, giving feedback, probing and listening, solving problems, and giving encouragement—will help you successfully handle almost any situation. Additionally, these skills are referred to in every chapter, each of which describes situations common to the workplace. Many of those situations come from experience; others come from actual court cases. My book, *Fair, Square, and Legal* (AMACOM, 1991), contains many of these.

The "Key Phrases" insets highlight useful questions or comments in those situations. For example, when giving feedback, you might use the phrase, "It seems to me . . ." to preface your opinion or feelings.

Each scenario begins with a brief explanation of why certain words are used or why certain steps are taken; or they might list steps you can take. It is followed by a note explaining the situation and describing the people featured in the dialog. Since the scripts aren't playlets that stand on their own, *please read these explanations before diving into the scripts.*

Many different characters populate this book, but one character remains constant: "You." "You" is you, the reader. The scenario will tell you what's going on and describe the other person or the people involved, and the script will draw you into the situation, but only you can make it all come alive. Read the part of "You" as if it *really* were you. But don't stop there. Read every script at least twice. The first time, take the part of "You." The second time through, switch roles. See how it feels to walk a mile in the moccasins of the other person. That will help you understand why some people may be defensive or aggressive, and it will help you understand how the suggestions in the script can make you feel better about how you are handling the situation. That's how you want the other person to feel, too.

Sometimes you may think the lines are a bit stilted—not the way people usually talk. You're right. My objective is to set out suggestions that get results, not familiar words. In fact, often the way people usually speak gets them into more trouble than they were in to begin with.

Don't be surprised that many suggested "things to say" are questions. Questions let you control the discussion or dialog by keeping the other person in your agenda and at your pace. Getting the other person to talk may be the best way for you to make your point.

Silence may be the best way of communicating in some situations. It's not always what you say that counts as much as the outcome you achieve, especially when you're engaged in mutual problem solving or decision making. As the old adage says, "Rather than give people your fish, teach them how to fish for themselves."

If time allows you to practice the roles with someone else, first play "You." Then ask for feedback. Ask the other person to tell you:

- What he liked
- What he didn't like
- What you could do differently

And here are some specifics to look for:

- How did I sound? (Was my voice too shrill or strident? Was I too loud? Too soft? Too harsh? Too wishy-washy?)
- Did I emphasize my main points? (Did my tone of voice convey what I felt as well as what I meant?)
- How did I look? (Was my posture intimidating, too close to the other person? Was I gesturing appropriately with my hands? Did my face communicate what I felt as well as what I meant?)

After getting the feedback, practice again if there is time. Then play the other part to see how it feels to be in that role. If your partner wants feedback about how she did, give her some.

If you have video equipment, role play for the camera. You couldn't ask for better feedback than matching what you see with what your partner says. Just answer the same questions I listed above.

Section I

Fundamentals Of Managing Discussions: Communicating, Giving Feedback, Problem Solving, And Encouraging

Most of the scripts in this book depend on your ability to give and receive feedback, to hold productive conversations in which you identify and solve problems or encourage others to do better. Your success at all supervisory functions depends in large part on how well you manage your discussions with others. Mastering these communication skills will increase your abilities to coach, counsel, correct behavior, conduct performance reviews, interview prospective employees, and build relationships with other people.

Chapter 1

Four Basic Steps To Effective Communication

Whenever you hold a discussion with someone, especially if you're discussing a problem, the following steps will lead to an effective or productive conclusion:

1. *Openers*
   a. Set the other person at ease with a warm and friendly manner.
   b. Identify the purpose of the meeting.
   c. Review the meeting's agenda (if you have one).
   d. Get the other person's commitment to looking at the situation (e.g., a performance problem or a career move) and taking the necessary steps.
2. *The Exchange (getting and giving information)*
   a. Ensure the accuracy of what you think or feel.
   b. Get information you may be lacking.
   c. Find out what obstacles you might have to manage if the person doesn't agree with you that a problem exists or if he feels angry or bad about the situation.
3. *Resolution of Differences (if any)*
   a. Identify the points of agreement.
   b. Summarize the differences.
   c. Use the points of agreement to negotiate a mutually satisfactory conclusion.

If a change is anticipated, a fourth step is appropriate:

4. *The Action Plan*
   a. Encourage the other person to design the plan, when possible.

b. Coach and guide without imposing solutions when you're helping another person solve a problem.
c. Come to consensus on (1) the plan, (2) the steps for implementing the plan, and (3) the steps for monitoring progress.

Disagreeing with the Boss—The Ideal Situation

Scenario—Reluctant Boss

Your department has been assigned two projects you believe have interfered with the whole division's success. You don't know why they were assigned to your group in the first place, since they both lie pretty far outside the group's competencies. Yesterday, when you told Margaret, your boss, that you wanted to talk about the projects, she seemed tense and resistant.

You set the stage for dealing with this disagreement with Openers that create an atmosphere in which problems can be solved. The atmosphere will largely determine whether you can persuade Margaret to do something about the problem.

Key Phrases
Openers

"I'd like to talk about. . . ."
"Let's review. . . ."
"I have a problem, and I'd like your help to. . . ."
"I asked for this meeting because I'd like us to talk about. . . ."
"I'm concerned about . . . and I'd like us to deal with it before. . . ."

You [*smiling, friendly*]:   Good morning. I appreciate your making time for me.

Margaret [*motioning for you to sit at the conference table and taking the chair next to you*]:   No problem. I've been meaning to talk with you anyway. I like the work you and your staff did on the Smith project.

You: Your memo to the chairman was very complimentary. Opening the doors the way you did made it a lot easier, too. But, Margaret, I asked for this meeting because I'd like to talk about the Phillips and Jones projects.

Margaret [*showing her tension with the topic*]: I've cleared forty-five minutes for you. That enough time?

You: I think so. It really depends on whether we can easily resolve a difference of opinion here.

Margaret [*stiffening*]: On what?

You: We're heading into the next quarter behind schedule and off target, and I think it's to everyone's benefit to re-examine what kind of work we take on and how we assign that work.

Margaret [*clearly not pleased*]: You're questioning my decisions?

You [*pleasantly*]: I'd like to make clear a few things from the start. One, this isn't a question of blame; I'm not pointing a finger at anyone. Two, I'd like to know what you think about the division's showing. Three, I'm offering a suggestion that I'd like you to consider. And, four, my interest is helping the whole division out of its hole. How do you feel about what I've said?

Margaret [*smiling*]: I guess you're reading my mind.

You: No. I just put myself in your shoes.

Margaret [*relaxing a bit*]: I appreciate that.

Disagreeing with the Boss—The Exchange

Tense, nervous, or suspicious people don't always unwind during the Openers stage of the discussion. In this case, it's often necessary to continually reassure them by letting them do the talking. For example:

- Ask for their opinions about the situation.
- Let them tell you about their feelings, including how they feel about talking about the situation.
- Practice the three *L*'s: Listen, Listen, Listen.

- Make sure the other person has said all he wants to say and has nothing more to add before taking your turn to express yourself or to give information about what you think or feel.
- Point out where the two of you agree as well as where you disagree to help pave the way to the next stage: Resolving Differences.

Scenario—Defensive Boss

Margaret still seems very tense. She may not be ready to listen to you. Letting her talk first will help you to find out why she seems upset. Once you understand, you can address those issues as well as your original point.

Key Phrases
The Exchange

Getting information (Gatekeepers)

"Tell me what you think about. . . ."
"How do you feel about . . . ?"
"What do you think is responsible for . . . ?"
"What's happening with . . . ?"

Giving information

"It seems to me that. . . ."
"I have some figures here that. . . ."
"I agree with you when you say . . . , but, on the other hand, I also think that. . . ."
"In my opinion, . . ."

You: You haven't said much about it, but I'm sure the division's performance is bothering you.

Margaret [*sharply*]:   It is. I thought I'd made that pretty darn clear.

You: You've told us you're disturbed. But to tell the truth, I'm not sure you've communicated the level of your discomfort.

Margaret: I'm *very* worried.

You: And the Phillips and Jones projects?

Margaret: *Extremely* worried.

You: So am I.

Margaret: Okay. What's your point?

You: It seems to me we've taken on too many noncore projects. The Smith project is only one out of five, and it's the only one finished. Only two of the five, Smith included, fit with our mandate and our competencies. One project is barely peripheral, and two—Phillips and Jones—are way outside our scope.

Margaret: The chairman wants them, and he assigned them to us because he thinks only we can do them.

You: Maybe we can, but *should* we do them? Look at these figures, Margaret. Direct and opportunity costs offset both long-term and short-term payoffs from both projects. These two projects are eating us up. We've had to hire consultants for both of them because they're too far out of our reach. Our people have spent more time backgrounding the projects than working on anything else. I think we'd be better off subcontracting both projects and getting on with our core business.

Margaret: That's how you see it. Anything else?

You: No. That's my whole case in a nutshell, but I can lay out a more detailed scenario if you want. What do you think?

Margaret: The chairman doesn't want them subcontracted. He's afraid we'll lose the accounts.

You: How realistic is that fear?

Margaret: Not very, and I think he can be persuaded otherwise.

You: Then what else is bothering you?

Margaret [*after a moment's hesitation*]: The politics.

You: The politics?

Margaret: An outside board member has an interest in keeping the projects in-house. Subcontractors could be his competitors.

You: Let me make sure I understand you. We're doing these projects because the chairman's afraid of losing the accounts, and one of the outside directors has a vested interest in keeping these projects here. Is that right?

Margaret: You've got it.

You: If we can find a way around both of those issues, you'll carry a plan to move those projects out of here?

Margaret: Well—maybe.

Disagreeing with the Boss—Resolving Differences

When differences surface, deal with them. Letting them lie on the table without doing anything about them won't make them go away. Instead, the differences will skulk around until they have an opportunity to bite someone—usually you—in a most uncomfortable place.

Scenario—Still Reluctant Boss

You and Margaret have now both expressed your viewpoints. You know that Margaret is deeply concerned about the division's performance and that politics more than anything else blocks the way to getting control over the situation. You see a fundamental difference between your position—you think the chairman's two pet projects should be farmed out—and Margaret's—she doesn't want to make waves with the board.

Key Phrases
Resolving Differences

"Here's where we seem to agree. . . . And here's where we seem to disagree."

"I can't agree with what you're saying because. . . . What do you think about what I've said, and how do you feel about it?"

"I see these disagreements. . . . And I'd like to resolve them before we go on."

"What do you see as our main points of agreement and disagreement?"

"What do you think we can do to resolve this disagreement?"

You: Maybe?

Margaret: You'll have to find a way around the fears and the politics.

You: Let me make sure I understand what we agree on and where we disagree. Okay?

Margaret: Sure.

You: We agree that these projects have created a number of problems. We also agree that the division's performance will improve and everyone would benefit from farming them out. We disagree about what to do about the situation.

Margaret: Yes. I think your numbers speak for themselves, but I don't like the politics involved.

You: Tell me what you don't like about it.

Margaret [*hesitating*]: I don't like bucking the board.

You: I don't understand.

Margaret [*somewhat impatiently*]: Don't be naive. Do you think it's worth it to fight the chairman and the board?

You: You think our jobs would be at risk. Is that it? [*Margaret doesn't answer.*] So that's our disagreement? [*Margaret nods in agreement.*] I don't think our jobs will be in jeopardy if we can show the chairman and the board that our plan would benefit the company and them. I think they'll buy it if we make it more attractive to them to let us farm out the projects than to keep them in-house. I don't think I'm naive in saying that the director's company can outbid and outperform his competition, and he can excuse himself from the decision to prevent a conflict of interest.

Margaret [*thinking about it*]: You think you can make the case?

You: *We* can.

Margaret [*smiling*]: If you go down, I go down.

You [*also smiling*]: We won't go down. I think we'll come out looking really good on this, but if it blows up on us, I'll take the heat.

Disagreeing with the Boss—Action Planning

Action planning focuses on how to do something or how to accomplish some goal that will be mutually satisfying to you and the other person. Action planning has three steps:

1. Plan what to do (to correct a problem, take another career step, or whatever else your meeting is designed to accomplish).
2. If the plan is for something you expect the other person to do or to accomplish, let her do most of the planning; that's the only way you can expect to get a commitment to the plan.
3. If the other person can't come up with a plan, make some suggestions, but don't create the whole plan and hand it to her to execute.

Scenario—Reluctant But Willing Boss

You and Margaret agree on the problem; now it's time to design a solution to it.

Key Phrases
Action Planning

"What steps can you take to . . . ?"
"What can I do to help you . . . ?"
"How long will it take to . . . ?"
"What else do you need for . . . ?"
"What do you think of this idea?"
"If you think that'll work, what else can you do to follow up on it?"

You: You know the chairman and the directors better than I do. What do you suggest we do?

Margaret: I don't really know. I'd like to see your plan before committing myself to anything. Since you seem to be taking the lead on this, what do you propose?

You: Give me a day to come up with some answers for the directors.

Margaret: What do you need from me?

You: Play devil's advocate. First, give me a list of objections I can answer. Then let's meet in the morning to review and rehearse my scenario and to edit it. Third, get me a meeting with the chairman. What do you think?

Margaret: I can do the first two. The third—well, let's wait and see what you come up with.

You: Fair enough.

Conclusion

Using the four-step method I described produces change. At the same time, it reinforces the other person's self-esteem because it isn't accusatory or punitive. But you have to plan the changes in appropriate increments in order not to overwhelm people with impossible demands. That's where effective problem solving comes in, the topic of Chapter 3.

Chapter 2

Giving Feedback

What if, in the middle of a conversation, the other person just up and says to you, "You're a liar"? That would bring some color to your cheeks, I'll bet. As my Texas friends say, "Them's fightin' words." But if the other person had said, "I don't think that's correct," you might still get upset, but you probably would be more willing to discuss the difference of opinion. Whereas the first statement might be "fightin' words"—an accusation rather than feedback—the second response is feedback in the form of information. It leaves you room to say, "Oh. I guess I was mistaken."

Positioning Feedback—The Ideal Situation

Feedback tells the other person how her behavior affects you and how you feel about it. It also asks her to change the behavior in order to prevent what happened from reoccurring. Complete feedback also includes a reference to consequences: What could happen if the behavior changes? What could happen if it doesn't?

Successful feedback depends on:

- How you position it
- How you deliver it

Miss the mark on either one, and feedback could turn into a struggle for survival.

When you position feedback, take the following points into consideration:

- People receiving the feedback must be at least willing to accept it, even if they don't seek it out.

- People who are properly approached will listen to your reactions to what they do or say.
- Unless people are willing to listen, you'll merely talk *at* them rather than *with* them.

Scenario—The Ideal Situation

You have an employee, John, whose work is usually above average and who is friendly and cooperative. Lately he has missed a few deadlines. That's a problem because your customers as well as other departments in the company depend on your department's timeliness.

Key Phrases
Giving Feedback

"It seems to me. . . ."
"I believe. . . ."
"The way I see it. . . ."
"I'd like to see. . . ."
"It may be to your benefit. . . ." [*WIIFM—or What's in It for Me?*]
"How do you see the situation?"
"How do you feel about what I've said?"
"What do you think we can do?"

You: Good morning, John. How are you?

John: Good. How are you?

You: Fine, thanks. I wanted to talk with you today about a situation that seems to be developing, and I thought we'd get control over it now, before it got out of hand. Is this a good time to talk about it?

John: As good as any other. Am I in trouble over something?

You: Not at all. It's just a matter of a few deadlines. You know how important it is that we meet them.

Positioning Feedback—Defensive Employee

Before giving feedback, you have to consider the other person's needs—both work-related and emotional—and be prepared to provide him with "benefit" statements (the WIIFM). People become more receptive to feedback when it meets their needs. At the same time, don't neglect your own needs. Since you have to recognize your rights as well as theirs, it's essential that the feedback meet both the other person's needs *and* yours. To do this:

- Position the feedback as a problem *you* have that the other person can help you solve.
- Use I-statements to prevent your feedback from becoming an attack on the other person or from being perceived as one.
- Assert yourself (don't be wishy-washy). Be honest and direct but not brutal and uncaring. Say, "I think," "I feel," "I want."
- Avoid You-statements that label or appear to attack the other person: "You are," "You never," "You always." (Avoid "you" statements with positive as well as negative feedback.)
- Describe specific, observable behaviors—*not* personality traits—over which the other person has some control.
- Deal with matters of concern to you about which you have personal knowledge or about which you have information you've checked for accuracy.
- Respond quickly to events.
- While giving feedback, check out whether the other person agrees with your facts or opinions.
- Mirror (reflect) feelings to ensure emotional needs are met also, and paraphrase what the other person says to check out the accuracy of what you're hearing.
- Involve the other person. Allow him room to contribute to the solution to the problem and to agree or not agree to do something.
- Spell out the consequences of inaction as well as the benefits of action.

- Be receptive to receiving feedback, even if you hear things you'd rather not.
- Guard against defensiveness or being argumentative.

Scenario—Defensive Employee

Same situation, but this time the employee is Fred, and he's not friendly and cooperative. Rather, he's somewhat surly and can be arrogant. You have to get his attention with a fairly strong statement and make it worth his while to talk about the problem.

Key Phrases
Four Parts of an I-Statement

"This morning I heard you say. . . ." [*what you experience or perceive*]

"I felt very. . . ." [*what you feel about it; what you like or don't like and why*]

"In the future, I'd feel a whole lot better. . . ." [*what you would like to see happen differently in the future (what you need from the other person)*]

"If it happens again, I'll have to. . . ." [*the consequences if things don't change*]

You: Good morning, Fred. How are you?

Fred: Good. How are you?

You: Fine, thanks. I wanted to talk with you today about a situation we seem to have developing that's creating a problem for our customers, for me, and for you. I thought we'd get control over it now, before it got out of hand, or put you or the department in a jam. I'd like us to take a bit of time to talk about it.

Fred [*brusquely*]: I'm very busy. It'll just have to wait.

You [*calmly*]: It'll take only a few minutes, and solving the problem can save you a great deal of time and perhaps some real grief later on.

Fred [*his attention captured*]: What's this about?

You: The quality of your reports is excellent, but there's a matter of timeliness. I've received complaints that you've missed several deadlines recently. Are you aware of that?

Fred: I missed a few by a day or two. No big deal.

You [*mirroring*]:   It seems that you feel put upon by this.

Fred: I just don't understand what all the fuss is about.

You: You know how important the deadlines are to our customers, and therefore how important they are to our department. When you miss them, it reflects badly on your performance, and I'd hate to see your reviews lowered by this.

Fred: I sent them memos about the delays.

You: According to these two memos, you missed the deadlines for the systems department twice in the last two weeks, both by two days. And last week, you missed the billing department's by three days. Is that right?

Fred: Yeah, I suppose so. I gave them notice that the reports would be late. They should've prepared better for that.

You [*paraphrasing*]:   Then you're saying that giving them notice that the reports would be late should be sufficient for satisfying their needs?

Fred: Why not?

You: Over the past two years you've held this position, you've never missed a deadline before. What's been happening?

Fred: I don't see what the big deal is.

You: If you miss deadlines, what happens down the line? [*Fred shrugs.*] C'mon, Fred. You know very well what happens.

Fred: All right. They miss their deadlines. But they don't have to. They can make up the time.

You: How?

Fred: Once they get their reports, they can make up the time.

You: Through extra work? You wouldn't like it if that happened to you, would you?

Fred: I guess not.

You: Fred, it's a problem for all of us, including you, but you don't seem willing to even discuss this with me. I'd like your help, first to identify the problem and then to solve it. It's to your benefit to work with me on it.

Fred: You're right. Look. I think I have too many projects on my plate. Check out that production board. I haven't a chance to breathe.

You [*paraphrasing*]: You think you have too many projects assigned to you?

Fred: Yes.

You: Do you think we should review the work distribution in the department?

Fred: That's a good starting place. Look, if you—you're letting my two co-workers off the hook and piling too much work on me.

You [*paraphrasing and mirroring*]: If I understand you, you think I'm favoring the other two people in the department at your expense and that makes you angry.

Fred: That's *exactly* what you're doing. And yes, it's making me damn angry!

You: If you think I'm favoring other people, I think we'd better talk about it.

I see your production board is loaded up, but I also see that everyone is equally loaded. The real issue, as I see it, is whether you can meet your deadlines, given the workload, and if not, what we can do about it.

I can see why you feel overloaded, but since everyone else feels they are, too, I don't appreciate it when you accuse me of favoritism.

Fred: Well, maybe I exaggerated a little, but I feel overwhelmed.

You: I understand the workload's heavy right now, and we do need to make some changes. All I'm asking of you is cooperation. Help solve the problem rather than lose your temper. Is that okay with you?

[*When Fred doesn't answer*] If you help us out on this, we may be able to redistribute the work in some way that is agreeable to you and that will help you meet your deadlines. If you don't cooperate, I'll probably redistribute the work in some way you still don't like, and we'll be in the same fix we're in now.

And, as I said, it'll reflect badly on all of us—but especially for you. What do you say, Fred? Going to work this out with me?

Conclusion

I-statements guide your feedback to the proper targets: behaviors, feelings, and desired results. To use them effectively, you have to aim them properly. Emphasize what you see, hear, and feel rather than what the other person does or says, and explain how it affects you or how you perform a task.

Giving feedback makes your position, your feelings or emotions, and your reasoning explicit. It helps other people to understand what's important to you, and it gives them a glimpse of what your reality looks like to you. At the same time, the feedback you give has to consider the other person's needs and feelings as well. My favorite Native American proverb is on the mark here: "To give a person dignity is above all things."

Chapter 3
Problem Solving

"It makes a problem," the young auto mechanic in Luxembourg kept repeating to me over the telephone. I had called his auto rental agency to report that the car I had rented in Brussels had broken down on the highway outside town. He couldn't speak much English, I couldn't speak much French, and the car was barely running. Worse, the English-speaking agency manager was out with the tow truck on another call, his return time unknown. Yes, it made a problem.

Identifying a symptom of your problem is usually what you do when you give negative feedback, like the feedback I gave the agency about the automobile's performance. The feedback described what the car had done: "The car I rented from your agency in Brussels has broken down." The problem I was asking the other person to help me solve was: "I need someone out here to get it running right or tow it in."

You aren't required to give negative feedback if things work out. The description of what does not match expectations or goals is the feedback. The problem is finding a way to make reality and expectations meet. And often, the difficulty revolves around essential issues such as beliefs, attitudes, values—or goals, like the goal of getting to Luxembourg in a disabled car.

Problems that involve differences of opinions or matters of fact are usually resolved by reference to facts. But to resolve problems that involve differences in attitudes, values, or goals requires careful management and even more careful use of your problem-solving and communication skills.

The scripts in this chapter show you how to cut through the symptoms of problems to causes and develop creative, mutually satisfying solutions.

Identifying Problems—The Ideal Situation

Follow these six essential steps of problem solving. If you leave out one piece of this process or take the steps out of sequence, you'll probably create another problem.

1. Identify the real problem or the real need by separating symptoms from causes.
2. Consider alternative solutions.
3. Agree on which solution to try first.
4. Implement the plan.
5. Monitor progress and the results.
6. If the first effort doesn't work, suggest another alternative.

Scenario—The Ideal Situation

Ordinarily Alice is very courteous and helpful to customers, but during the past three weeks, several older customers have complained about her rudeness and inattention. When you speak with her, the conversation goes well.

Key Phrases
Separating Symptoms and Causes

"What seems to be happening?"
"How often does it happen?"
"When doesn't it happen?"
"Where does it happen?"
"What should be happening?"
"Who's involved when it happens?"
"Who isn't involved but should be when it happens?"

You: These complaints disturb me. They're not like you. What's been happening?

Alice: I can understand your concern. As you said, these things have happened only in the last three weeks. I didn't get complaints before.

You: Why are they coming now?

Alice: A personal problem with my mother. That's probably why I'm short with the older women. I thought I had it under control, but I suppose I haven't done as good a job as I thought.

You: Other people have complained, but it's true—most of the complaints have come from older women. What do you think we can do about it?

Alice: Well, maybe I can try to. . . .

Identifying Problems—Uncooperative Employee, Part 1

Step 1 of problem solving—identifying the real problem or need by separating symptoms from causes—often generates the solution as well. Don't underestimate the power of problem identification, especially when you're working with an uncooperative person. Until she sees that a problem does exist, she'll resist any attempt to change the situation.

Most people look at the surface of the situation and call what they see the problem; in reality, though, they're only seeing the results or the symptoms of the actual problem. Five steps can help you make the leap from a fuzzy guess to a more confident probability. Sometimes you may be able to jump from Step 1 to Step 5, but that's rare.

1. *Collect initial data.* What's happening? What should be happening? The scripts all start with an undesirable solution; reality doesn't match the ideal, a sure sign a problem exists.

2. *Formulate the initial statement of the problem.* This statement focuses on the relationship between what should be and what is—for example, "I should not be making as many errors as I am, missing so many deadlines, and arguing with people."

3. *Collect additional data.* Now find out all you can about your situation by asking open-ended questions, questions that begin with *who, what, why, where, when,* and *how* and that help you flesh out the details you need for talking with the other person.

Open-ended questions do just what the name implies: They open the gate to information or to discussion. (These questions are also called *gatekeepers*.) You can't answer them with a simple "yes" or "no" or "maybe," the way you can with closed-ended questions that begin, "Are you," "Can you," "Do you," "Have you," "Is it." Any question that can be answered with a yes or no or maybe merely confirms information or, worse, puts an end to a discussion.

4. *Identify contributing factors.* After collecting the information, identify factors that contribute to the discrepancy between what is and what should be.

5. *Formulate the final statement of the problem.* State the problem as the relationship between what is happening and the contributing factors. On the basis of this statement, you'll be able to list alternative solutions to the problems.

Scenario—Uncooperative Employee, Part 1

For the last three weeks, Carol has been making numerous errors, missing deadlines, and arguing with other employees. She has complained to others that you are always "on her case." After she comes into the office, you first have to gain Carol's cooperation.

Key Phrases
The 80/20 Rule

"Tell me what you think is happening." The rule here is to listen 80 percent of the time. Ask as many questions as are necessary.

"Let me tell you what I think." The second part of the rule is to talk 20 percent of the time. Be concise and to the point.

You: I've heard you're unhappy with me.

Carol: Can't anyone around here keep quiet?

You: You're upset that someone told me you're unhappy with me.

Carol: Wouldn't you be?

You: I'd just like to find out if it's true, and, if it is, what's happening. Then we can resolve the issues and get on with our work.

Carol [*surprised*]: You're not mad at me for talking behind your back?

You: I'm not happy about it. I'd rather you talk directly to me, identify the problem, and get it under control.

Carol [*after a pregnant silence*]: You've been nagging me about my work lately. That's the problem.

You [*after another pregnant silence*]: I'm nagging you. That's the whole problem, as you see it?

Carol: That's how it is.

You: I agree that I've talked to you about your work a lot more recently than I ever have before, but I wonder if that's the real problem.

Carol: You call it talking. I call it nagging.

You: Let's take a closer look. Maybe that'll help us identify the real problem and get at the root cause. Willing to give this a chance?

Carol: Sure.

You: When do I talk with you about these matters?

Carol: It seems as if it's all the time.

You: How often does it really happen?

Carol: A couple of times a week, I guess.

You: Was there ever a time I didn't seem to be nagging you?

Carol: Well, sure. It's been only lately. Since you're not nagging anyone else, I think you've got a beef with me.

You: If I did, why wouldn't I just come out and tell you about it?

Carol: So you're saying that you're not mad at me about anything?

You: I'm not mad at you. I'm upset about errors, missed deadlines, and arguments. Still, my anger's not the issue. I don't think the errors, the deadlines, or the spats are the problem, either. I think they're just symptoms of something else.

Carol: See! You *are* blaming me.

You: I'm just saying that you're making more errors and missing more deadlines than you used to. Agreed?

Carol [*reluctantly*]:   I suppose so.

You: I want to know why they're happening. The errors and missed deadlines started popping up about three weeks ago. What changed?

Carol: I don't know. [*After a pregnant silence:*] I started using the new word processing package—the one corporate wants every-one to use.

You: Who else is using it?

Carol: Everyone. But I seem to be having more trouble with it than the others. I'm an expert in our old system. This new system—that's another story.

You: And it may be the source of our problem here, too.

Carol: What do you mean?

You: You were expert with the old system, but this new one seems to be throwing you. How?

Carol: The key commands aren't the same. Setting up columns is different. It does more things than the old system, but I don't know all it can do. I spend a lot of time looking in the manual to do everyday sorts of stuff, and I'm still reading about its capabili-ties. Other people have said the same things.

You: Didn't the training help?

Carol: We had a half-day orientation. That's all. I don't think it was enough, and I don't think it covered the right things. I'm strug-gling with the system. I make lots of errors and miss deadlines. Then I get frustrated and snap at people. Since I didn't tell you what's going on, you get on my—I mean, you give me feedback that I take to be nagging. Get on track, and my problem goes away.

Solving Problems—Uncooperative Employee, Part 2

When considering alternative solutions:

1. Look at more than one way to solve a problem or meet a need.

2. Involve the other person as much as possible.
3. Offer suggestions only if the other person cannot.

Scenario—Uncooperative Employee, Part 2

Carol admits to the problem she has—she can't work the system—and to the collateral problems she is creating—errors, missed deadlines, arguments. Now she has to come up with the solution.

Key Phrases
Looking for Alternatives

"What do you think we can do to . . . ?"
"What do you think of this idea?"
"I think we might try. . . ."
"What else, if anything, can we do?"
"Let's consider these options."
"So these are the options. One, ..."

You: How do you think we can get things turned around?

Carol: That's up to me, I guess. I need to learn to use the system.

You: And how do you intend to do that?

Carol: I'd like to take the manual home to study, but I can't load that package on my computer. It takes more memory than mine has. So that won't work. Maybe I can stay late and work on it.

You: You know how the boss feels about overtime.

Carol: Do it on my *own* time here and *not* get paid for it! At least at home, I could do other things, too. [*pregnant silence*] The college has one-day computer courses, and some have a couple of levels for this system, too. I could go to the intermediate or advanced class on this. It'll be just one day, but I think it'll be worth it. Would the company pay for it?

You: Doesn't the software company offer more training?

Carol: When the company came in, they said that was all the training we got. We can get technical assistance over the phone, but it takes forever to get through, and then they only untangle one problem at a time. You don't think the company would pay for the class, do you?

You: Maybe through tuition reimbursement. Or maybe I could talk with my boss and see about pulling it out of our training budget. How much do the classes cost?

Carol: I don't know. Last year they ran around $120. Some of the other people might want to take the courses, too. What if we talked with the college about sending a teacher over here? We could set up the computers in the third-floor classroom, where we had the orientation. Maybe we can cut a deal to get the per-head cost down some.

You: I can talk with the boss about it.

Carol: Would it help if all of us asked for it? We all can use it.

You: That sounds okay, but understand that we can't pull everyone off at once.

Carol: What if some of us go? Get the training, come back, and train the others.

You: Sounds as if we have several options. You work on it here on your own time, or you go to class at the college, or the college sends someone here to train everyone, or some of you get the training and train the others.

Carol: Which do you think would fly?

You: We'll have to price the alternatives. I'll give the business school a call this afternoon. Then I'll take all four options upstairs.

Solving Problems—Uncooperative Employee, Part 3

When determining which solution to try first:

1. Arrive at a consensus rather merely assume you and the other person agree on everything.
2. Get a commitment from the other person to make an effort to correct the situation.
3. Make a commitment to work on the solution too.

Scenario—Uncooperative Employee, Part 3

If you carry the four options upstairs without agreeing on what appears to be the best solution, you could be in for a very unhappy surprise later. You and Carol spend the next few minutes working on her commitment to the change.

Key Phrases
Agreeing on a Tentative Plan

"Which idea do you like best?"
"Let's weigh the alternatives and decide on the basis of. . . ."
"Then it's agreed? We'll do . . . first."

Options 2 and 3 can be backup plans.

You: Which idea do you like best?

Carol: That some of us go for the training and come back and teach the others.

You: Do you think you can handle that yourself—only you go for the training and come back and teach the others? That's a fifth option.

Carol: Yeah. I think I can handle it—if everyone isn't mad at me for being grouchy the past few weeks.

You: That's the option I like most, and I think that's the one that will fly best. [*Slight pause:*] So what do you think we've accomplished?

Carol: We solved my problem, and I'm not mad at you anymore. I don't think you're just nagging me either. The real problem is the new system and my lack of expertise with it.

You: That's good. Now let's get on with our work.

Solving Problems—Uncooperative Employee, Part 4

Act on your decisions, or they will be hollow and meaningless (and you'll lose face with the other person).

Scenario: Uncooperative Employee, Part 4

The next day, you bring some decisions from upstairs.

You: I talked with the boss. We've agreed that you can go to the class at the college and then coach the others, two at a time. We can take the cost out of the training budget.

Carol: What about having the teacher come here?

You: The college wouldn't reduce the price any, and the training budget's not big enough to cover it. Also, sending two or three of you would be too expensive.

Carol: I thought it seemed too easy.

You: Nothing you shouldn't have expected. Do your best to keep up with your work, although I'll shift some of it over to the others for the time being. The next class starts in two weeks.

Carol: In the meantime?

You: You'll just have to struggle along. Then if the class doesn't help you get up to speed, we'll have to send someone else to study the system and to come back and fill your role. That could affect your performance review, so there's some risk to you to do this. We need a separate backup plan for handling errors and missed deadlines if all doesn't go well.

Carol: And if all goes well?

You: You mean, what's in it for you? Besides that I quit nagging you?

Carol: Sure.

You: Well, I can't offer you a raise, but I can offer you lunch at your favorite restaurant—at least a favorite restaurant I can afford.

Carol: You're on. [*Slight pause:*] I wouldn't like to get a bad review or to lose my job, so if I'm still having trouble after the class, I'll stay late to practice. Is that okay?

You: That seems to be a reasonable backup plan.

Solving Problems—Uncooperative Employee, Part 5

Action without follow-up is also as hollow as no action at all. Once you have a plan:

1. Monitor its progress and results.
2. Observe or measure when and how reality and expectations meet. The goal is for performance to match standards.

Scenario—Uncooperative Employee, Part 5

Several weeks later, you and Carol have another discussion about Carol's progress.

You: The class seems to have helped you—over a week with no errors, you're back on your deadlines, and you haven't snapped at anyone. And you've done a lot to help the others as well.

Carol: I think I'm a pretty good teacher, if I say so myself.

You: They think so too, and so do I. Pick your restaurant.

Solving Problems—Uncooperative Employee, Part 6

Not every story has a happy ending. The first "solution" may not work. In that case, try again with a backup alternative.

Scenario—Uncooperative Employee, Part 6

In our original story about Carol, all's well that ends well. Had it not ended as it did, other steps would have to have been taken. Let's see what might have happened.

You: It's been two weeks since you took the class, and you still seem to be struggling with the system. The errors and the missed deadlines haven't improved. In fact, if you look at the numbers, they seem to be heading down.

Carol: I guess that means I don't get to teach a class for the others.

You: I'm afraid not. It also means that we have to figure out exactly what your problem with the system is. I don't want to have to put you on probation, but if the errors and missed deadlines continue, I'll have to do that.

Carol: Then I'll start snapping at people again. [*Pregnant silence:*]
      Yeah, I know, I've been snapping already.

You: You're feeling pretty bad about this.

Carol: Yes. I know I'm not cutting it on the new system. We'll have
      to put my backup into motion.

You: We're sending someone else to school. You can get the extra
      coaching from her, and—

Carol: Yeah, I know. Practice. Practice. Practice.

Conclusion

Working with employees to identify the causes of problems and
alternative solutions produces more effective results than does imposing solutions and demands from above—and it takes a great
deal of stress out of your job.

     The six-step method of problem solving—identifying the
causes of problems, sifting through the possibilities, settling on a
tentative plan, implementing and monitoring the plan, and taking
corrective action when necessary—supports the manager's job and
effort. Effective feedback and the language of collaboration will get
you through most common difficulties.

Chapter 4

Encouraging Others

How do you encourage other people to "keep a stiff upper lip" (as the British say) when the sky seems to darken above you as well as them? What do you say to help:

- Shy or withdrawn people to talk?
- A promising employee with a job performance problem?
- An employee with a personal problem that's interfering with work?
- Survivors of a downsizing program that has put an extra burden on them?

Most important, in every case, surface feelings and deal with them. Suppressed problems or negative feelings interfere with relationships, create barriers to productivity, and throw obstacles into the path of growth and development.

Yet a lot of people say that you shouldn't get involved with emotional issues, that feelings don't have a place in the workplace, and that personal issues don't play any role in business relationships. Many people refuse to deal with negative emotions (affect), regardless of the potential cost. Some feel threatened by personal or emotional issues; expressions of feelings or emotions threaten their security and disrupt the workplace. Don't rock the boat, they say, and everything will be okay. Additionally, many people believe that feelings and emotions, especially their own, are private and personal—and not anyone else's business.

It's true. Some personal matters (pertaining to family, health, friendships) shouldn't be a part of business—unless performance and working relationships suffer because of them. Then you must address them or pay serious consequences later.

Our first principle here is that *the whole person comes to work,* and a whole person is a delicate balance of perception, knowledge, skill, emotions, and feelings—a balance easily undone by seemingly minor events. When symptoms first emerge (e.g., reluctance to participate, frequent tardiness or absenteeism, quick anger, and other undesirable behaviors), it's time to become an encourager.

An encourager opens the gate, so to speak, for other people to go through. Open-ended gatekeepers encourage others to open up about personal problems or feelings. Positive feedback, even as you're taking corrective action, encourages people to commit to making an effort to change. Lending an ear, pitching in, reinforcing good feelings, and rewarding achievements help people feel that it's all worth the effort. That's what this chapter is about.

Encouraging a Withdrawn Person to Open Up—The Ideal Situation

Encouragers help others experience their own worth. They have confidence that the other people will succeed at what they're doing, and they have confidence in themselves and in their ability to help them do it. Encouragers use a number of subtle devices to work their magic:

- Open-ended questions—those that begin with *what, which, why, when, where, who, whom,* and *how*—and open-ended comments (e.g., "Tell me more")—encourage the other person to talk about or elaborate on something. Open-ended questions or comments encourage other people to talk or to express themselves. They are especially useful for people trying to solve a problem or people who tend to be uncommunicative by nature. None of these gatekeepers that probe for information or for clarification can be answered "yes" or "no."

- Mirroring (reflecting feelings), allows people to talk about their feelings and emotions, negative or positive. This device helps people work through disagreements or conflicts, and it helps you encourage withdrawn people to open up.

- Paraphrasing can elicit more information or clarification (by paraphrasing and then asking, "Is that right?").

• Pregnant silence (or the Law of Productive Nothingness), helps the other person decide whether to answer. In some cases, it leads to self-discovery or problem solving. When using pregnant silence, ask a question or make a comment, and then wait for an answer. You are giving the other person an opportunity to think, to speak, or to respond. In all probability, she will fill in the silence—unless you fill it instead.

Scenario—The Ideal Situation

Tom keeps to himself a great deal, doesn't volunteer much conversation with anyone, and tends to answer questions with one word, usually "yes" or "no." He's a good worker too. But now the company has mandated that all units organize into closely knit functional teams. The team-building classes seem to have helped everyone in the group rise to the challenge—everyone but Tom, that is. His manner makes everyone uncomfortable, and he doesn't contribute much to problem-solving discussions. As team leader, you have to do something about it, so you invite him to lunch away from the company commissary.

Key Phrases
Open-Ended Gatekeepers

"What do you think of . . . ?"
"When do you feel that . . . ?"
"Why do you think this is important?"
"Where can you get the information you need?"
"Who else is . . . ?"
"How do you feel about . . . ?"
"Tell me more about. . . ."
"Give a complete picture of how you see things."

You: I'm glad you accepted my lunch invitation.

Tom: It's a free lunch. Why not?

You: Well, you've probably figured out that I have an agenda. I want to talk about how you see things in this new team environment and get some idea of how you feel about participating more. How do you feel about talking about those things?

Tom: I suppose it's okay.

You: You have no problem with it then.

Tom: No.

You: What *do* you think and feel about the team concept?

Tom: [*after a pause*] It's okay, I guess. [*pregnant silence*] I'm not used to it. Never worked that way before. Give me a job, tell me what you expect, and let me do it. That's the way it's supposed to be.

You: If I understand you, you really don't like working in and with a team.

Tom: No, I didn't say that. It's not what I'm used to, that's all.

You: Tell me more about what that means to you.

Tom: Working with other people is fine, but I'm not comfortable complaining about who is doing what or not doing it. If there's a problem, fix it; don't sit around talking about it. Mostly it's a waste of time.

You: You mean, things we do in the team seem to waste time? What can we do to make you more comfortable?

Tom: Well, since you asked. . . .

Encouraging a Withdrawn Person to Open Up—Difficult Situation, Part 1

Encouragers listen well. They:

- Listen to what other people say and how they say it.
- Give out sincere compliments when they're earned.
- Treat others with respect.

Scenario—Difficult Situation, Part 1

The situation is essentially the same, only now Tom is *not* cooperative. You listen to Tom's feelings as well as his words and compliment him appropriately. You respect Tom's feelings and ask him to talk about what he wants to talk about. In this way, you get Tom to talk about how he feels about the teams.

Key Phrases
Mirroring

"I sense that you're. . . ."
"From the frown I see on your face, I guess you're feeling. . . ."
"What am I really hearing in your tone of voice?"
"When you talk that way, it seems as if you're. . . ."

You: I'm glad you accepted my lunch invitation.

Tom: It's a free lunch. Why not?

You: Well, you've probably figured out that I have an agenda. I want to talk about how you see things in this new team environment and get some idea of how you feel about participating more. How do you feel about talking about those things?

Tom: I don't think I want to.

You: You'd rather not talk about it with me?

Tom: No. I'd rather not talk about it. Period.

You: Then let's talk about *why* you don't want to talk about it. It's important to me to know what you're thinking and feeling.

Tom: Why? What's it to you?

You: The easy answer is that I'm team leader, but that's not the whole of it. You're a good worker, Tom. People could benefit from your experience and training—and from your work ethic, I might add. And, finally, I'm genuinely concerned for your welfare, as I am for everyone else's. How do you feel about my reasons for wanting to talk?

Tom: I'd rather you let me be.

You: What can I do to encourage you to participate more, at least in this conversation?

Tom: I have to admit, you're persistent.

You: I am. How do you feel about that?

Tom [*smiling*]: I'm not much of a talker, but you're bound and determined to make me one.

You [*smiling back*]: Yes, I am. What do you want to talk about?

Tom [*after a pregnant silence*]: Why'd they go and form these teams?

You: You don't like the teams.

Tom: Well, I guess they're all right, but I'm not used to them. I never worked that way before. Give me a job, tell me what you expect, and let me do it. That's the way it's supposed to be.

You: If I understand you, you really don't like working in and with a team.

Tom: No, I didn't say that. It's not what I'm used to, that's all.

You: Tell me more about what that means to you.

Tom: Working with other people is fine, but I'm not comfortable complaining about who is doing what—or *not* doing it. If there's a problem, fix it; don't sit around talking about it. Mostly it's a waste of time.

You: You mean that things we do in the team to you to waste time? What can we do to make you more comfortable?

Tom: Well, since you asked. . . .

Encouraging a Withdrawn Person to Open Up—Difficult Situation, Part 2

Encouragers give useful corrective feedback, then support the other person's self-esteem, even when giving negative feedback, which is as important, at times, as positive feedback. You don't help someone by overlooking his shortcomings, regardless of what they may be. Also, the effectiveness of feedback concerning areas in need of improvement depends not only on *what* you say but also on *how* you say it.

Scenario—Difficult Situation, Part 2

You have encouraged Tom to talk, and now you want to enlist his support for the team.

Key Phrases
Giving Effective Corrective Feedback

"I like the way you did . . . I'd like to suggest, if I may, another way of doing it."

"I felt pretty bad when you said . . . I suppose I would have been more receptive if you had phrased it differently."

"Your opinion is important to me; I just wish you wouldn't use coarse language when expressing it."

"Overall, except for two specific terms, I like the work you did on. . . ."

"This report shows a great deal of effort and attention to detail, but it's not ready for delivery. Let's look at what works and what's missing."

You: I appreciate what you're saying, Tom. I'm not all that used to a team approach either. Some of the things you've said make sense, and maybe we can adjust the team's process to accommodate them. At the same time, I don't agree with everything you said. Mind if I lay them out for you?

Tom: Well, you listened to me. It's only fair I do the same for you.

You: Two things. One, the weekly production meetings do produce results; you've seen the productivity charts yourself. The key difference from the old way is that we've found that some people are more skilled at some work than we thought. Two, contrary to what you said about not having much to say about things, you do. You're the most experienced person in the unit, and your opinion counts with everyone, including me. More than that, in the past you solved some important production problems. What do you think about my opinions?

Tom: Well, I've seen the charts, and I hear what you say, but—to be honest—I think you're trying to manipulate me.

You: What makes you think that?

Tom: You're greasing me with talk about my experience. I don't see why anyone would listen to me.

You: Why do you think we wouldn't?

Tom: There isn't one of you that doesn't have more education than I do. You know that I never finished high school; everything I know, I learned right here on the floor. Most of you will go on to higher positions in the company or in some other company, and I'll still be here looking after these machines and getting this work done.

You: You think we don't respect you because we're better educated.

Tom: That's what I think.

You: What else is bothering you?

Tom [*surprised*]:   What do you mean, "What else"? That's enough. I shouldn't have said that much.

You: Okay. You think we believe we can't learn from you because we've finished high school and some of us, including me, went to college? Tom, I could argue with you about this until the cows come home, but only by becoming a real part of the group will you ever see that it's not true. We all believe we can learn from you. But I think something else's is bothering you—that you're nursing a sore or something.

Tom [*reluctantly*]:   Whatever it is, it's my problem to handle.

You: As long as it interferes with how you work with the team, it's my problem too.

Tom [*still reluctantly*]:   It's nothing I can't handle by myself.

You: Tom . . . ?

Tom: Yeah, you're concerned for my welfare, and you're darn persistent. [*After a pregnant silence:*] I'm older than all of you, and I've got some problems that come with getting older—aches and pains, that's all.

You: If that were all, I don't think you'd be reluctant to talk about it. Tom, I might be able to help.

Tom: Nah. It's physical. The doctor says I've got some heart blockage—you know, angina. It hurts some, but he's got me on medication and says I'll be fine as long as I exercise and watch my diet. Doesn't recommend surgery or anything, but . . .

You [*after a pause*]:   But you're worried about it anyway. Right?

Tom: A little.

You: I'd be a little worried, too. But it doesn't seem to have affected your work.

Tom: Nah. I sit at the machine most of the time. But I guess it's affected my mood. I get moody, you know.

You: Yes. I know.

Tom: Okay. You win. I'll try to lighten up on you guys. You'll see a difference in how I work with the team.

You: No, Tom. *We* win. We're teammates, right?

Encouraging a Withdrawn Person to Open Up—Difficult Situation, Part 3

Encouragers see and express the up sides of down situations. They:

- Help people work through difficult situations, especially situations that create stress or barriers to success.
- Promote change, improvement, growth, and development, and express enthusiasm for what they and others are doing.
- Encourage an ongoing communication once they get other people to open up that continues to reinforce their good feelings.

Scenario—Difficult Situation, Part 3

Tom has opened up with the real problem—the illness that has him more worried than he'll admit. You have to reassure him that it will not affect his relationship to the group or affect his job.

Key Phrases
Encouragement

"I feel good about what you're doing."
"It's not an easy job, but I'm confident you can do it."
"You must feel good about how you're doing."
"You're making progress."

"I like what I see."

"Your . . . in the face of . . . means a lot."

You: I don't know how severe your heart disease is, so I'm not going to say things like "Everything'll be all right," or "Hang in there, pal," or any of those other movie lines. I only know that we need you, and I think you could use our support right now. That's what teamwork is all about, isn't it?

Tom: I suppose.

You: Thanks for telling me what's happening. It'll be easier for me to understand what's going on now.

Tom: It's just between us, right?

You: Between us only.

Tom: Not the team, not your boss, not Human Resources.

You: As long as you don't get really sick, it's our secret. You have my word on it. But, Tom, you have to make me a promise, too.

Tom: What?

You: If your angina gets worse and you need help, you'll ask for it, and you'll let me go to Human Resources to get what help they can give you. You have to tell me what's happening and let me do what I can and have to do. Promise?

Tom: Promise.

Conclusion

Dealing with the whole person—feelings, emotions, and job skills—pays. If you ignore any of these facets, they can sabotage everyone's performance. When giving a performance review to a below-standard producer, consider how he's feeling. When an otherwise good performer's work suddenly deteriorates, there is usually a personal problem, a skill problem, or a knowledge problem lurking beneath the surface. Deal with emotions when they interfere with work.

Open-ended questions encourage people to talk, and they indicate that you want to hear what they have to say. Mirroring, too, encourages others to talk about their feelings or emotions, and it indicates that you care about what they feel. Creating a positive climate keeps people energized. Being an encourager makes you feel good, too.

Section II

Interviewing Prospective Employees and New Employee Orientation

All through this book, I script dialogs that include questioning techniques, but none are more specific or directed than questions used while interviewing prospective employees. And none raise more red flags to which managers need to pay particular attention than do these questions or comments. Probes about health or personal matters, about non-job-related issues, or about gender-related experiences have little or no place in a job interview, and many questions during an investigation can be out of line or slanted.

Equal employment opportunity laws have a bearing on how you can interview prospects, as do other laws (including the Americans with Disabilities Act, laws of contract, and privacy laws). Although I don't review the legal issues, I do show you how to probe sensitive areas without getting into trouble. (My book *Fair, Square, and Legal* [AMACOM, 1991] goes into more detail about safe interviewing practices.)

The first three days of a new employee's experience in a company are the most important. As many exit interviews attest, the first impressions last forever. The first three days mean a lot to the company as well; they largely determine how well the employee will perform on the job. To help you make these three days count, I provide ways to introduce the new employee to the work group, explain how to provide her with a context in which to work, and explain how to create an effective psychological contract between you and the new employee.

Chapter 5

Interviewing Prospective Employees

What are we looking for when we recruit new employees? Too often, people hire on the basis of chemistry ("It feels right") or because the applicant reflects their image ("She's just like me"). One way to keep personal chemistry and reflections out of the picture is to take a committee approach to interviewing and making hiring decisions. But even so, you still have to interview people to see if they have:

- The skills necessary for doing the job.
- The education or training that provides them with those skills or that demonstrates their capability of learning them.
- The personal characteristics that fit in your environment and culture.

These categories, listed in order of importance, guide everything you do from preparation for interviewing to the hiring decision.

An axiom of the personnel business is that past history is an indicator of future success—so consider each applicant's work history first. Many independent factors may have contributed to a good or a poor performance on another job, but the right questions about what the person did in previous positions will tell you whether the person has the specific skills or transferable skills needed to do your job. Most important, previous work history will show whether the person has the kind of work habits you want. (Don't overlook work in the home or the volunteer work that a large number of women entering the workforce have done.)

Look at the applicant's educational history next, and distinguish between formal education and skill training. Formal education focuses on knowledge and understanding, not doing, and a college degree may not be as valuable as on-the-job training in some cases. Balance questions about book learning against questions about learning how to do things, which may take place outside the formal classroom (e.g., skill training or leadership training).

"Chemistry" does play a role in the interview process but not only the personal chemistry between interviewer and applicant. A skilled, educated candidate could turn out to be absolutely wrong for the job if his personal history doesn't fit into your culture or the job or the people he'll have to work with. How a candidate works with others, gets along with them, and communicates with them lets you know more about him than do reference checks. How the person responds to supervision, success, failure, constructive disagreement, and conflict also reveals the person. Some of the relevant questions relate to a person's family background; such questions are permissible as long as they are clearly job related, are asked of every candidate for a specific job, and don't have an adverse impact on any particular group of persons.

Let's say the job calls for assuming personal responsibility for certain tasks (for example, closing out the register and locking it up at night) with limited or no supervision. Then, when interviewing someone without a work history, you might ask him what family responsibilities he has had to assume. Or when the job calls for managing a budget, you could ask a woman coming into the workforce after raising a family about her experiences with managing a budget.

Use the four-step method for the interview: (1) set the candidate at ease, (2) conduct the interview, (3) summarize your impressions, and (4) explain the next step in the process.

Interviewing for a New Employee—Qualified But Shy Applicant

Before launching a recruitment campaign, know what the position is and what it entails. Building your interview guide on that basis will keep you on track and improve the quality of your hiring decision. Start the process by following these guidelines:

- Develop a functional position description based on goals (results required and the standards by which job performance will be judged), tasks, and activities essential to the performance of the job. Include realistic, achievable, measurable, or observable results expected and activities and methods requiring to achieve those results.
- Collaborate with employees currently doing the job and with your personnel staff to write the job description and task analysis.
- Devise an interview guide or plan that includes the right questions for digging out the information you want.

In the interview itself, heed these guidelines:

- Be prepared, because questions help you control the exchange. Be spontaneous only in response to the answers you get to your prepared questions.
- Analyze the resume carefully. Question any gaps in the record, for example, and look for hidden skills training (e.g., as in military experience). Use the resume as a basis for formulating questions.
- Set the stage, but don't prime the candidate's pump by describing the position beyond what is public knowledge (for example, in the classified ad).

Scenario—Qualified But Shy Applicant

An experienced, apparently highly competent graduate of an executive secretarial program, Charles Smith, applies for the position of sales secretary. He operates both IBM-compatible and Macintosh systems: desktop publishing, word processing, spreadsheets, the works. He also takes dictation and operates dictation equipment. What a gem—on paper. You find out the quiet side of this candidate during the first interview and have to level with him rather than keep him waiting until you hire someone else.

Key Phrases
Interview Questions

"The job calls for. . . . What have you done in previous jobs like this?"

"The job calls for. . . . How do you feel about doing that?"

"The job requires. . . . Tell me about your successes in this."

"Our organization has. . . . Please describe your experiences with this in the past."

". . . is an essential function of the job. Have you ever had a problem doing that, and how did you feel then?"

You: I'm pleased you accepted my invitation to interview with us, Charles. Would you like something to drink? Coffee? A soft drink?

Charles: No thanks.

You: Today is just a preliminary interview. We'll talk mainly about what you've done, and how you did it, that fits with our job requirements—your work history, education, job preferences, things like that. Okay?

Charles: Sure.

You: First, what about our advertisement led you to send in your resume?

Charles: You're looking for someone who can work on a PC.

You: Yes, we are. Why does that interest you?

Charles: I've worked on both IBM and Macintosh systems. Top in my class and for a year in my last job.

You: What specifically did you do in your last job?

Charles: It's in my resume and on my application.

You: Yes, that's true, but I'd like to hear you talk about your work— what you liked the most, disliked the most, things like that.

Charles: I like working the Mac for desktop publishing, but for ordinary word processing and spreadsheets, I like the IBM better.

You [*after a very pregnant silence*]: On your last job, what kind of environment did you work in?

Charles: Excuse me?

You: The environment. Did you work closely with other people, or did you work more or less on your own? Did you have much contact with customers? Those sorts of things.

Charles: Well, mostly I worked by myself. Sometimes I worked with other people, but I rarely had contact with customers.

You: Which did you like better: working by yourself or working with other people?

Charles: By myself.

You: Charles, the title of this position is sales secretary. What does that mean to you?

Charles: I guess that means being a secretary to salespeople.

You: Doing what?

Charles: Typing letters. Keeping records. The ad said something about putting out a newsletter.

You: Those things are parts of the job, but the ad also said that you'd be working closely with a sales team; taking calls from customers—and sometimes they're angry calls—calling customers, activities that result in customer satisfaction and that require a *lot* of people contact. How do you feel about that?

Charles: I guess I can handle it.

You: I'm not sure that you have the amount of people contact experience we need. You're highly skilled in what you do, and if this weren't such a public job, I'd probably want to hire you, but I have to be direct and up-front with you, Charles: I don't think you'd fit into this position.

Interviewing for a New Employee—A Perfect Fit, Part 1

The kinds of questions you ask determine the answers you get. Knowing what the job requires helps you make decisions based on the answers that candidates give to very direct, job-related questions. The amount of talking you do also determines the quality of the interview itself. These guidelines will help you conduct the interview:

- Avoid putting unnecessary pressure on the candidate that doesn't reflect the pressures of the job for which the candidate is interviewing.
- Apply the 20 percent rule: The interviewer should talk no more than 20 percent of the time. The more gatekeepers you use (e.g., open-ended questions or comments), the more you guide and control the direction of the interview.
- Use either-or questions (a form of closed-ended question) to help you sort out an applicant's values, attitudes, and preferences, as well as help pinpoint information you want. ("If you had a choice, would you rather play a team sport, like baseball, or be in a one-to-one competition, like figure skating?")
- Use laundry lists to help get additional information, especially if the applicant doesn't understand your question.
- Don't be vague ("Tell me about yourself.") or ask leading questions ("You like working with machines, don't you?").

Scenario—A Perfect Fit, Part 1

The second candidate, Carla Lopez, has excellent skills (IBM and Macintosh) and experience as a sales secretary. Carla also impressed you with how she handled herself during the telephone interview to set up the appointment. She asked questions that would help her prepare for the interview, probing specifically about the needs of the sales group with which she would be working.

Key Phrases
Probing for Information

"What on your last job did you find most enjoyable?"
"What did you enjoy least?"
"How much experience have you had with . . . ?"
"What kinds of experience have you had with. . . ?"
"If you have a choice between . . . or . . . , which would you prefer?
"What leisure activities interest you the most—sports, TV, reading, movies, something else?"

You: I'm pleased you accepted my invitation to interview with us, Carla. Would you like something to drink? Coffee? A soft drink?

Carla: No thanks.

You: Today is just a preliminary interview. We'll talk mainly about what you've done, and how you did it, that fits with our job requirements—your work history, education, job preferences, things like that. Okay?

Carla: Sure.

You: First, what about our advertisement led you to send in your resumé?

Carla: As I said on the phone, the company where I'm working as a sales secretary now is going out of business the first of the month, so I'm looking for a new job. Customer contact is an important part of what I do, and your ad made it clear that this position has a lot of customer contact. If I had to sit in front a computer all day, typing letters, I'd be bored.

You: So you enjoy dealing with customers. What do you like about it?

Carla: Knowing that I'm helping both the company and the customer meet its needs. [*laughing*] I guess maybe I should've been a social worker, but that's the way I was raised: to help people.

You: The job does call for a lot of time in front of the computer too. How do you feel about that?

Carla: That's okay as long as it's not the only thing I do.

You: How about working with the team? What's your experience with teamwork, off the job as well as on the job?

Carla: Off the job?

You: Yes. What kind of teamwork situations have you been involved in, and what did you do?

Carla: Well, in high school, I was on a softball team. And—oh yes—I was the chairperson of a dance committee, in my senior year. How could I have forgotten that!

You: You seem to think that was quite an experience.

Carla: It sure was. There were nine of us on that committee—an odd number just in case we needed a tie breaker. And did we ever! No one could ever agree on anything! I wanted to make it an event we'd remember all our lives, and I think we succeeded—but not in the way I wanted.

You: How's that?

Carla: It was a disaster. Nothing was done on time. I was still in my jeans, hanging crepe paper and balloons when people began arriving.

You: Sounds as if you didn't enjoy working on the committee.

Carla: Not that one! [*After a slight pause:*] I'm a team player. Everyone will tell you that. But maybe I'm not cut out to be a team leader. There's a big difference, you know.

You: Tell me about the differences.

Carla: As I said, I like to help people. I like taking on an assignment the team needs done, make my contribution. The leader has to pull it all together, keep everyone working together, manage all the little details, make too many decisions that upset people. I'd rather not hassle with all that.

Interviewing for a New Employee—A Perfect Fit, Part 2

Theater people tell you there are great readers and great actors, and the two may not always be the same person. Someone who auditions well may turn out to be a terrible performer. The same is true of interviewing for a job. During a first interview, you see the cover of the book, the best foot forward, the halo. (Pick your own cliché.) Take care you don't fall into a hiring trap based on a first, and perhaps only, impression. Instead, don't make commitments during a first interview; leave some questions unanswered and bring back at least three candidates for second interviews. Another way to avoid the "halo effect" of first impressions is to get a second (or third) opinion on the applicant.

Scenario—A Perfect Fit, Part 2

Carla is a hit. She's the first of three candidates you have called back for a second interview.

Key Phrases
The Second Interview

"During our first interview, you said. . . . I'd like you to tell me more about that."

"Let's take a closer look at what you might be doing here. How would you . . . ?"

"Here's a problem we have. . . . How would you go about tackling it?"

"To be sure you and we make the right decisions, we'd like you to spend time talking with some of our people and look over the place. How do you feel about that?"

You: Thanks for coming back to see me today, Carla. You changed your hair, and I hardly recognized you. It looks very good.

Carla: Thank you. People told me that my hair style made me look too young—not as professional as I wanted to look. I was afraid this was too severe, so thanks for noticing.

You: It does make you look a little older, but I wasn't put off by your appearance before, so I'm not the one to judge. [*After a slight pause:*] I'd like to talk some more about what you'd be doing here if we were to offer you the position—see what you think about some of the problems you'd have to handle and what you think you could do to help us with some important issues in the department.

Carla: That's great! I did a little homework, and I see that the company's expanding very rapidly. That could put some pressure on the sales department, especially if you're adding salespeople. As the sales secretary, I'd have my hands full.

You: Yes, you would. In fact, that's one of my questions for you. The phone rings a lot at the sales secretary's desk—customers calling to see if their orders have been processed, account executives calling in rush orders. Sometimes you have two or three lines lighting up at once.

Carla [*not waiting for the question*]: That happens a lot on my job now—lots of calls, mainly customer complaints, but salespeople calling in for quotes as well as rush orders. Just yesterday, a sales-person called in for a quote at about 10:30, and the customer called in the afternoon wanting to know if the order was shipped yet!

You: How did you handle that?

Carla: I didn't know if the order had even been placed. Where I work, orders are placed in the distribution center, not in the sales office. I don't usually get the information until after the order is filled. That's what I told the customer. Then I got her phone number, checked out the order, and called her back. It was a rush job and the order had been filled, but we were waiting for the carrier to pick it up.

You: What did the customer say when you called her back?

Carla: My ear still blue? She really let me have it—like it was my fault. I wonder what she's going to do when she finds out the company is going belly-up.

You: She doesn't know?

Carla: No. I've been told not to tell anyone. An announcement's going out next week. The employees have known for a long time—a legal requirement or something—but our customers don't know. Management is afraid that the customers will bug out on us, and we'd be in bigger trouble than we already are.

You: That shows a lot of loyalty to the company, and it also shows you can keep a confidence, but I'm curious: How do you feel about this situation?

Carla: Not good, but the boss said not to tell, and I do what the boss says. So has everyone else, I guess. Our paychecks depend on what little business is coming in.

You: Then you don't have a problem withholding important information from your customers?

Carla: It bothers me some, but what can I do? [*After a pregnant silence:*] There's probably a better way of handling this, but I don't make the decisions. I'm just following orders.

You: I see. What have you said to your boss about it?

Carla: "Aye, aye, Captain." It's management's call, not mine.

You: You haven't given him any feedback or expressed your feelings about this?

Carla [*puzzled, even alarmed*]: Is this a problem for you?

You: How do you feel about disagreeing with people in authority?

Carla: What do you mean?

You: Let's say I do something you don't like—maybe make a decision that rubs you the wrong way. What would you do or say?

Carla [*face reddening*]: What *can* I say? I know what you're getting at. You think I should've spoken up about withholding information from the customers.

You [*pleasantly*]: That's not for me to say. I'm more concerned about how you would react to something I or this company does.

Carla [*relaxing but still guarded*]: Oh, I see. [*Taking a deep breath:*] I'm not used to what you're asking for. At this place where I'm working, people don't like their decisions questioned by subordinates. I'd have to get used to speaking up, and I guess I'd need some prodding, but I'd do it if that's expected.

You: As you know, we call people who work here "employees," or "staffers," or "associates"—or we use their titles. We *don't* have "subordinates" here. And, yes, it's expected that people speak their minds because that increases our confidence in our decisions and in having our decisions carried out. Carla, in our organization, employee suggestions and feedback are very important. We define loyalty not only in terms of keeping company confidences but also in terms of speaking up if you think there's a better way of doing something. We'd *expect* you to speak up if you thought we did something wrong or that we could something better. How do you feel about that?

Carla [*brightening*]: Sure, I could do that, if I'm given the chance. It's just not done where I am now.

You: Then you think that under different circumstances, you could act differently.

Carla: Definitely. And it's because you've said that's what you expect. I know what'll happen to me if I contradicted my boss now.

Interviewing for a New Supervisor—Reasons For Rejection

Work experience and personal characteristics often mean more than education when hiring a new supervisor than when hiring line employees. What the supervisor has done, how successful he has been at it, and how well he relates to other people become paramount. When interviewing for a supervisor:

- Ask questions about previous experiences, not just about hands-on work experience.
- Check out each candidate's knowledge of equal employment opportunity requirements.
- Examine each candidate's previous experience managing people with diverse backgrounds.
- Determine if each candidate's management philosophy fits with your organization's.

Scenario—Reasons for Rejection

You've been looking for a production supervisor for nearly a month. The person in this position is expected to supervise men and women with a diversity of ethnic and racial backgrounds. In fact, some of the employees speak English as a second language. It has been difficult to find someone with the right work and supervisory experience, as the interview with Hank suggests.

Key Phrases
Interviewing for a Supervisory Position

"In previous supervisory positions, how did you handle a situation in which . . . ?"

"What do you think are a supervisor's primary responsibilities?"

"A special order requires you to ask for Saturday overtime. An employee balks on religious grounds. What do you do?"

"Several employees speak English as a second language. What do you do if . . . ?"

"What experiences have you had working with minorities?"
"We can't always find people trained to fill our jobs. How do you feel about training new employees? What experience have you had training and coaching employees?"

You: If you get the position, we're going to have to add two more people to the line to keep up with sales orders. How would you go about recruiting the people we need?

Hank: No problem. I've been in the business a long time. I can get you the guys you need.

You: "The guys"?

Hank: Yeah. I know some men who'd jump at the chance to work here.

You: We have a job posting system here. An affirmative action program, too.

Hank: I know; so did the last place I worked. But to get the best people, the bosses looked the other way when we brought in our own kind.

You: "Your own kind."

Hank: You know. Journeymen. People who know the job. People who can speak and read English, too.

You: How do you feel about supervising people whose second language is English?

Hank: Well, I've supervised some Latins. They're okay, but we don't always have time to explain things they don't understand. It's better if we have people who speak English as good as I do.

Interviewing for a New Supervisor—Hiring the Right Supervisor

Good answers to tough questions and good reports from other people lead to making an offer. In the interview:

- Answer questions directly, honestly, and forthrightly.
- Don't promise anything not authorized by your company in

a way that could be construed as a binding contract. You and your company could get into serious problems if the company can't or won't deliver on unauthorized promises.

- Protect yourself and the company from potential lawsuits by asking only questions that are specifically job related and asked of everyone. Avoid unwelcome remarks that can be construed as intimidation or harassment (e.g., "We've never had a person of your [race/religion/gender/etc.] working here").

Interviews are appraisals in which you're attempting to judge whether the applicant fits your organization. It's the best fit (the whole person) you're looking for, not merely the best qualified.

Scenario—Hiring the Right Supervisor

After talking with eight people with previous supervisory experience, you interview Lorna; she has the right work history, the appropriate supervisory experience, and some of the people skills you're looking for. Others have been impressed by her as well. You call her back for a final interview because you have some unanswered questions, and you need to find out how serious she is about the job. After exchanging appropriate small talk, you get on with the interview.

Key Phrases
Hiring Interview

"Let's talk about a few unanswered questions I have."
"What do you think and how do you feel about the materials that describe the company?"
"What unanswered questions do you have about the company?"
"What questions about the kind of future you can have here do you want to ask?"
"Let me tell you a little more about the company."
"We'd like to extend an offer to you. How soon do you think you can respond?"

You: We've talked about your experiences supervising minority employees, and since we last spoke, we've hired a person with physical disabilities in another department, so that raised a question in our minds about your experience with people with disabilities.

Lorna: I've never supervised anyone with a disability. None of my other employers hired any.

You: How do you feel about supervising someone like the woman we hired last week? She's in a wheelchair.

Lorna: Can she do the job?

You: Yes.

Lorna: Then what's the problem? My only concern is if she can do the job for which she's hired. What did you do to make her workplace accessible to her?

You: What do you mean?

Lorna: Did you have to rearrange the furniture or anything?

You: A little. And we had to ask other people to help her get supplies from the higher shelves in the unit. No one minds doing that.

Lorna: As I said, what's the problem?

You: No problem. We just had to see how you fit in with our philosophy of hiring only on the basis of job-related skills regardless of the person's physical challenges. [*After a pause:*] If we made an offer this morning, you think you'd accept it?

Lorna: I think so. I might want to think it over for a day or two, but that depends on answers to some questions I have, too.

You: Such as?

Lorna: Just some questions about benefits and pay raises and such. I've jotted down four of them based on what I read in the materials you gave me. Dependent coverage—who pays? The deductible on the medical insurance—how much per family member? When would I be eligible for a pay raise? And where can I go in this company after I've spent a few years in this one department?

You: The first two are easy. The employee pays for dependent coverage. The per person deductible is $500. On a slightly related subject, we will require you to take a physical examination if we offer you the position—mainly because some of the work involves chemicals that could have serious consequences if you have a pulmonary condition of any kind. Also, because public safety's involved, the Department of Transportation requires that all employees take a urine test. How do you feel about a physical exam and a urine test?

Lorna: No problem there, either. I know I don't have pulmonary problems because I've worked around these chemicals most of my adult life, and I know I don't use illegal drugs. So, it's okay—as long as you require the exams of all new employees.

You: Yes, we do. [*pause*] As to pay increases, the first one would come after the three-month probation period. The position pays $2,500 a month now; after ninety days, if you pass the probationary period, you'd get an automatic increase to $2,750. After that, your increases depend on your performance evaluations, your seniority, and other factors, such as production bonuses. After two years, you'll be eligible for the savings plan, in which the company matches your deposits one to one. After three years, you'll be eligible for our profit-sharing program. How do you respond to those conditions?

Lorna: Fine. I especially like the production bonuses and the savings and profit-sharing plans. It'll be the first time I've worked for a company offering them.

You: The last question is the hardest one: where you could go from here. [*slight pause*] Lorna, we never promise a new employee more than what we think we can deliver. The benefits are good because the CEO wants them, but we don't have a sophisticated human resources program here—in fact, no human resources department. Still, we do try to promote from within. Everything really depends on what we need, when we need it, and what you can do to meet those needs at that time.

Lorna: No career path, then? I really would like to move into higher levels of management.

You: No career paths as such, but after you've been around here a while, you'll know what other jobs there are that appeal to you. The more you know about those jobs and how to perform them, the more likely it is that you'll move into one. Some of the moves might be lateral, with no pay adjustments; some might be at a higher pay level. It all depends on the job. As for promotions, if you want to get into management, we'll have to see what you can do with leadership roles.

Conclusion

Making the right hiring decision saves the company the expense of replacing that person later. More than that, the right decision can make the company money or at least improve the bottom line.

You could also cost the company a great deal of money if you don't interview properly. In several places in the dialogs, the interviewer could have stepped into a discrimination lawsuit by saying or asking the wrong things. The interviewer might have told Charles Smith, "We want a woman in this job," or could have asked Carla Lopez, "You're Mexican, aren't you?" or "You speak Spanish, don't you?" The question asked of Carla seems innocent, but it isn't job related, so do not ask it.

The manager also refrained from asking about Lorna's dependents when the opportunity arose. How many dependents, the state of their health—none of that is relevant to the company at this time. They become relevant only if Lorna is hired and enrolls in the medical benefits program.

The same is true with regard to the state of Lorna's health. Because nothing about Lorna will prevent her from performing the essential functions of the job, questions about health apply only to enrolling an employee in the medical benefits program. And if the insurance waives restrictions on prior conditions, the questions aren't relevant either.

Making the right decisions and hiring the right people is a major part of a professional manager's job.

Chapter 6

Providing Effective Orientation

Too many managers think that a brief lecture and question-and-answer session about employee benefits and company policies are all a new employee needs to be oriented to the organization. They fail to realize that even experienced but new-to-the-company employees need to feel that they're not just another social security number. They need:

- Information about their roles and expectations
- Reassurance about their position and their security
- An introduction to the company and to the work group that makes them feel welcome

Sending them home, after the hiring interview, with an employee handbook is not enough.

There is no formula for an effective employee orientation, but these elements are basic:

- A discussion of the employee handbook.
- A personal introduction to the managers and coworkers with whom the employee will have significant dealings. In small- to medium-sized companies, the introductions should include senior managers and the CEO.
- A detailed discussion of the job and the expectations that both you and the employee have of one another.
- Appropriate training if the new employee is also new to the skills, demands, standards, and requirements of the job.

The last two elements should also be included if the employee transfers from another department in the organization into yours.

Creating a Psychological Contract—Reassuring A New Employee

At the heart of the psychological contract between you and your employee lies a detailed discussion of the job and the expectations that you and the employee have of one another. Regardless of whatever legal contracts exist, an employee's relationship to his job, to his coworkers, to you, and to the company depends on what he perceives you expect of him and what he can expect from you and from the company. In your discussion, make sure you cover the following points:

- Provide a written job description, and discuss the job in detail.
- Set reasonable, realistic, and measurable or observable standards on which both you and the employee can agree.
- Offer to help the employee to adjust to the new position. Keep your promises.
- Ask for questions or concerns, and respond to them honestly.
- Make realistic promises concerning the employee's security and future with the company—promises that the company can deliver on.

Scenario—Reassuring a New Employee

John has been a journeyman machine operator for over ten years; recently he was laid off when one of the company's competitors went under. When he interviewed with you, he expressed little interest in management, although he thought he'd like to get involved in new employee training someday. If he is as good with the machines as he says, that could be a likely road for him to follow.

Key Phrases
Orientation

"What questions do you have about. . . ?"

"How can I help you. . . ?"

"What do you feel you still need to know about. . . ?"

"Tell me what you think about. . . ."

"Let me tell you what I expect from you."

"What do you expect from me?"

"Let's talk about the employee handbook. What in it seems most important to you right now? [*Then:*] Let me tell you what I think is most important for me."

You: How was your visit with Human Resources this morning?

John: Good. The medical package offers more than my last one, and they answered a lot of questions for me. Cleared up a lot.

You: Any questions still hanging out there? Any loose ends?

John: No. But if I think of any, you'll be first to hear about them.

You: Now we need to talk about the unit and your position, and the expectations we'll have of one another. You've met everyone you'll be working with. Journeymen all. They know their jobs and have high standards. As I told you during your interviewing, I don't set the production standards for the unit; they do.

John: That's one of the things I heard that I liked.

You: They take a lot of pride in their work. Zero defects is the rule, not the exception. Their safety record is the best in the company, too. They work by the book in that regard. How do you feel about all that?

John: Great. If my last employer operated that way, I probably wouldn't be here. Their loss seems to be my gain.

You: I'm glad you feel that way. We all work hard here. Overtime is not uncommon, but it has its rewards. When you looked over the machinery this morning, did you see anything you're not familiar with?

John: No. It's all just about the same. I flipped through the operating manual, and I think I can step right up to it without any trouble.

You: Let me tell you my expectations for the first thirty days. . . .

Creating a Psychological Contract—Orientation For an Employee without Job Experience

Orientation usually goes smoothly and easily when the new employee knows the job. Change the scenario to a new employee with no experience in the job, and the orientation takes a lot more preparation, patience, and communication. During orientation for an inexperienced new employee:

- Set the employee at ease, understanding first-day jitters (nervousness that could produce a false bravado).
- Be precise and clear in your instructions.
- Stop frequently for a process check (to find out if the employee is on track with you and how she feels about things you're saying) to make sure you're communicating.
- Take your time. A thorough orientation could save you much time down the road.

Scenario—Orientation for an Employee Without Job Experience

The first time Jacqueline ever saw the machines on which she would be working was the day that she walked through the unit during the hiring process. She had had other manufacturing jobs but never with these machines. She's a quick study, she says (and so does her job history), and she expects to pick up the skills she needs easily. You had wanted to hire an experienced worker, but few qualified people applied; small budgets produce lean pickings. Still, Jacqueline seems eager and capable.

Key Phrases
Orientation

"Let me show you. . . ."
"Here are some things I think I ought to know."

"These are my expectations."
"What can I do to help?"
"What questions do you have?"

You: How was your visit with Human Resources this morning?

Jacqueline: Good. The medical package offers more than my last one, and they answered a lot of questions for me. Cleared up a lot.

You: Any questions still hanging out there, any loose ends?

Jacqueline: No. But, if I think of any, you'll be first to hear about them.

You: Now we need to talk about the unit and your position. You've met everyone you'll be working with. They are experienced people and know their jobs. They also have high standards. As I told you during your interviewing, I don't set the production standards for the unit. They do.

Jacqueline: I hope I can measure up.

You: Don't worry. Everyone knows you're new at this, and they meant it when they told you they'll do anything they can to help. Some people have been in this unit for a long time. They taught me the ropes when I came here, and I'm sure they'll take you under their wing, too.

Jacqueline: That's reassuring.

You: They take a lot of pride in their work. Zero defects is the rule, not the exception. Their safety record is the best in the company, too. They work by the book in that regard. How do you feel about all that?

Jacqueline: They understand that I'm new and will help me. What more can I ask for?

You: Let's take this discussion in three parts. First, we'll talk about the employee handbook I gave you to read. Then we'll talk about the job description I gave you. Third, we'll talk about what I expect from you and what you expect from me. Okay?

Jacqueline: Sure.

You: What's the most important thing in that handbook to you?

Jacqueline [*thinking about it*]:   I don't really know for sure, but a question I had concerned the family leave policy. I'm not sure I understand this—wait a minute, let me find it. Here. This paragraph about eligibility and the amount of time available.

You: Our plan goes beyond the minimum required by law. You're automatically eligible, but if something were to happen tomorrow—say, if your husband got sick and you had to take care of him—you wouldn't have enough time accrued to take as much leave as you'd need. You'd have to borrow against future vacation and sick leave time.

Jacqueline: Oh, I see. The longer I'm on the job, the more time I can bank.

You: That's it. The same is true about vacation time.

Jacqueline: Let's see. What else? [*pause*] Well, I'm glad to see policies that prohibit harassment. And I like the promotion-from-within policies.

You: What makes them important to you?

Jacqueline: As I told you during our interviews, we didn't have policies against harassment in a place where I worked just after I got out of high school.

You: I remember. You said you were approached often.

Jacqueline: The company didn't do anything to stop it either, so I quit.

You: I don't think that'll happen here. What about the promotion policy makes it important to you?

Jacqueline: I'd like to be a supervisor someday. I'm young and ambitious. My mom worked for seven different companies just to get two promotions, and both times she got them by changing jobs. I don't want that to happen to me.

You: Let me tell you how the system works. After you've been in one job for two years and get good performance ratings, you'll be eligible for a transfer. You might transfer laterally, or you could transfer up. Being a lead person in any unit will help your chances of being considered for supervisor.

Jacqueline: How come a couple of people have been in this unit for so many years?

You: Neither of them has a taste for management. They like what they do, take pride in what they do, and they'll continue doing it until they retire if they can. But it can be different for you. If you're good at what you do, take pride in it, and make an effort to learn and to grow, you could find yourself climbing that corporate ladder. No promises, mind you, but the possibility is there.

Jacqueline: What about more money? Don't they want to earn more money?

You: Without revealing confidential information, I can tell you that our technical ratings have provided them with a wage escalation clause that's the envy of the industry. One of our company's goals is to be included in the list of the nation's 100 best companies to work for. We're almost there.

Jacqueline: Looks like a lot of options.

You: There are. Anything else you want to talk about with regard to the handbook?

Jacqueline: No. That's it.

You: Let me tell you what's important to me. You'll be sent to the training unit tomorrow. Your instructor will show you everything you need to know about operating your machines. Don't be afraid to admit that you don't understand something. Your instructor expects that of you. He'll tell you, "There's only one stupid question." Jacqueline, do you know what that question is?

Jacqueline [*puzzled*]:   No.

You: It's the one you don't ask. I'll be checking on your progress daily, so let me know if you have any problems at all. At the end of the first week, you and I will meet to talk about how things are going. During that meeting, I expect you to tell me exactly how you feel, how you think you're doing, and what we can do to help you learn the job. This week is crucial to your success on the job, and I don't want anything to go wrong. We want you to be open with us immediately because we'll expect that openness all the time. How do you feel about being open with us?

Jacqueline: It'll be a new experience, but I like it.

You: So let's talk about your job. You have the printed job description, and I want to go over each step with you, alert you to what to expect in the training, and what I'll expect from you on the job. [*After they discuss the details of the job:*] Given all that, what can I do to help you adjust to this place?

Jacqueline: Nothing that I can think of, except you said you want me to speak up whenever I feel the need. Well, I'd like you to do the same. I don't want to be working along and thinking everything is just fine and find out in three months that I'm fired because I failed to meet the standards.

You: Don't worry. I'll let you know just how I see things going. Anything else?

Jacqueline: No. Well, maybe one more thing? Where's the nearest rest room?

Conclusion

The rapport you build with your new employees creates an aura of good feeling that lasts even through hard times—when the work seems to be piling up, when deadlines seem to be getting shorter, and when people seem to be all thumbs. Employee loyalty has been hard to come by lately, partly because of all the downsizing that went on in the late eighties and is still continuing. Employees feel less loyalty from their employers and give less loyalty.

You can help cement your employees' relationship to you if you see to it that they feel important to you and to the company from the beginning of their employment.

Section III

Performance Management: Reviews, Appraisals, and Coaching

A learning organization, Peter M. Senge says, defines the successful business of the future. Senge, the author of *The Fifth Discipline* (Doubleday, 1990), means that growth and development are an organizational state of mind—a culture that values continuous learning—not merely a periodic exercise for managers and their employees. Solving problems, making decisions, expanding product lines, and entering new markets depends on the ability of all employees to contribute to the business. The organization that fails to invest in training and development, in coaching its employees, will fall behind organizations that do make such investments. The twenty-first century will be won by the technologically and intellectually competent, not by the ignorant and unskilled. People who engage in continuous learning improve skills, upgrade quality, innovate or create new products, and provide exemplary customer service. Nothing—no machine, no artificial intelligence—can replace human knowledge and skill. Without them, machines cannot exist, and they would have no reason to exist.

By their very nature, educational institutions can't provide immediate response to the technological and economic changes they help produce. This is the chance for supervisors and managers to take the lead in the learning process and teach, train, coach, and counsel their employees.

Coaching employees, appraising employee performance, and taking corrective action are the key elements in the performance management system that is basic to any learning organization. How to execute that system is the subject of this section.

Although it may not be fashionable to talk about appraising employee performance, coaching is impossible without first deciding whether employee performance meets the standards to which you coach. An "Attaboy!" is as much an appraisal as "Shirley, you've reached 90 percent of our quality standard, and now we now have to figure out how to pick up that last by 10 percent." Without goals, objectives, and standards, you can't distinguish between praiseworthy deeds and areas in need of improvement.

Coaching is basic to a learning environment insofar as this activity:

- Helps or facilitates experience
- Involves problem-solving processes
- Provides decision-making opportunities
- Ends with a planning session

Effective coaches help people to improve their work or upgrade their skills, learn how to solve problems, and make decisions; they facilitate self-discovery and guide people to change the conditions of their lives.

You can't take corrective action unless you know what should be; this is the starting place for identifying problems and solving them. From a legal standpoint, the courts have ruled on numerous occasions that without performance standards and formal appraisals, disciplining or dismissing employees may provide grounds for claims of wrongdoing on the part of the employer. When coaching fails, formal corrective action, including dismissal, may be necessary, but you had better know what you're doing and why.

Chapter 7

Reviews and Appraisals

Performance appraisals come in many shapes, sizes, and styles. "You jerk! You did it wrong again!" is a performance appraisal (though not one that I recommend). So is, "Thanks to your efforts, we've increased customer satisfaction by 25 percent over the last survey. I appreciate all you've done." This appraisal uses the kind of appraisal language emphasized in this chapter.

A performance appraisal is any critical judgment or evaluation, positive or negative, of an employee's contribution. Measurable or observable goals, objectives, and standards form the results for which you hold employees accountable. Their inclusion makes evaluations objective; their absence makes evaluations arbitrarily subjective and open to challenge. Acceptable subjective language refers to your own perceptions and feelings but anchors them in measurable or observable objectives or standards.

An informal appraisal is any expression of approval or disapproval by supervisors or more experienced peers—the sorts of things you say when you make offhand remarks ("Attagirl!") and are almost always involved in coaching or counseling. Informal reviews are often event driven (e.g., a customer complaint); you coach and counsel without going through all the formal procedures of memo writing and other follow-up steps associated with formal appraisals. I recommend what some companies mandate: regularly scheduled informal reviews in which you and an employee chat from time to time about how things are going.

Whereas informal appraisals help you stay close to the employees' daily activities and reinforce motivation, formal appraisals do little to affect motivation; rather, formal appraisals are the culmination of the entire appraisal process. Usually a scheduled management requirement, a written document is produced, an interview time is set aside, and the interview is conducted. An appeal system and structured follow-up procedures are sometimes built into the process as well. But you can use the formal appraisal process at any time, especially when you need to take corrective action with regard to a persistent performance problem or a policy violation that demands intervention.

Since "You jerk! You did it wrong again!" is an unacceptable performance appraisal, it's up to you to make your performance reviews sound more like, "Thanks to your efforts, we've increased customer satisfaction by 25 percent over the last survey. I appreciate all you've done." Seven reasons support managing performance with ongoing informal and formal appraisals:

1. Continuous improvement (unless you measure it, you can't improve it)
2. Communication and recognition of contribution on the part of both employees and their supervisors
3. A clear demonstration of management interest in employees and enthusiasm for their achievements
4. Opportunities for rewards and for growth and development in the future
5. Mechanisms for managing performance (for monitoring performance, taking corrective action, and following up)
6. Documentation through performance management files, complete with memos and formal written appraisals, for digging deeper into a situation, highlighting serious consequences for poor performance, preventing trivial disputes or claims, and preventing the organization's losing a case on appeal
7. Showing cause for disciplinary action and providing a basis for promotion

Informal Review with Positive Feedback—The Ideal Situation

Informal reviews drive the performance management process; they also create the collaborative climate of the process and give the process its continuity. When you give a positive review, recognize the person's achievements, and let her claim credit for what she does right or well. Then reward real achievements appropriately.

Scenario—The Ideal Situation

A third very pleased and satisfied customer in as many weeks writes a note commending Dolores, a claim adjuster. The recent floods in her region have created extraordinary pressures on everyone, and Dolores seems to have risen to the challenges extremely well. You complimented her on both previous occasions, and now, after checking through those files, you discover that she also made settlements below her authority limits: Dolores not only satisfied the customers, she saved the company money in the process. To reward and recognize this performance, you compliment Dolores and offer her a growth opportunity.

Key Phrases
Effective Appraisal Language

Objective appraisal language

"Given your job standards, your performance. . . ."
"During the past three days, I've observed. . . ."
"Company rules state . . . and you have. . . ."
"You're to be commended for exceeding job standards by. . . ."

Acceptable subjective language

"Thanks—good job."
"I appreciate your efforts that have produced these results."
"I'm pleased by these results."

You: Dolores, I just received a third customer commendation letter about you. It seems that you're doing something *very* right. Good going!

Dolores: Thanks. That flood has been really hard for our customers to deal with. They need reassurance that things'll be all right and that we're here to help them.

You: What you do works—and you could have awarded higher amounts.

Dolores: I guess so, but after I talk with the claimants for a little while and we talk about their losses, that's all they ask for. No one's tried to gouge us, and I've never had to back anyone off a figure they requested.

You: What do you say to them?

Dolores: Whatever's right at the moment, I guess. I really don't have a set pattern. I just do what comes naturally.

You: That's pretty remarkable. Do you mind if we record your conversations—pick out a few of them to use as role models in a training session in the future? After you listen to your own tapes, you can put together a program for the session. It'll be one of those growth opportunities we're always looking for.

Dolores: I don't know that what I do is all that wonderful. Thanks for asking, but I don't know if I'd be much help. I might freeze up if I know I'm being taped.

You: What if I tape randomly? You'll know that your calls are subject to monitoring, so we'll be within our legal limits, but you'll never know which ones are being taped. That way, you can be yourself at all times.

Dolores: I guess so.

Informal Review with Negative Feedback—Reviewing Poor Performance

It's hard for supervisors and managers to give negative feedback. Recognizing that both giving and receiving negative reports bothers people, some companies no longer say *"negative* feedback." Now they call it *"corrective* feedback." (A rose with another name . . .) Yet negative feedback—telling someone that something is not good or acceptable—need not be punitive or demeaning. When it's time for you to give negative feedback, remember these points:

- Accent the positive but confront the negatives.
- Place the negative feedback into an objective context (e.g., customer complaints, production standards).
- Recognize the other person's feelings, concerns, and problems.
- Support the other person's self-esteem even as you discuss areas in which she needs to improve.
- Let the other person identify the problems and their causes, even if that means giving *you* negative feedback about what you have or have not done.
- Let the other person contribute to solving the problems.
- Spell out the consequences of not improving and the rewards for doing so.

Scenario—Reviewing Poor Performance

This past week, Janet, usually a top claim adjuster, has fallen behind on her file closings, and the backlog has produced complaints from customers, accounts payable, and upper management. You have to deliver this negative feedback to Janet, find out what is going on, and make plans to correct performance. Most of the employees in the unit take bad news pretty much in stride (and you can be direct with them); Janet doesn't usually take bad news very well. The key to success here is the concern for her that you show.

Key Phrases
Informal Review with Negative Feedback

"How do you feel about how things are going?"

"Let's talk about your progress toward. . . ."

"Given the standards, we need to take a look at how you're doing."

"I'm not happy with the way things are going."

"I'm very upset that you're not meeting the job standards."

"That you're violating company policy by . . . makes me very angry."

"Even though I'm pleased with how you're doing in, . . . I've some problems with. . . ."

"You seem to be doing very well in these [job performance areas], but there's room for improvement in. . . ."

"Given this situation, what do you think you can do to . . . ?"

You: Seems like the floods in your region have really inundated our offices. I don't think I've ever seen so much activity from the starting gun to the finishing bell.

Janet: Me neither.

You: What's your caseload like?

Janet: Pretty heavy. I can't see over my desk at all.

You: How you holding up?

Janet: Okay. I'm beat when I get home. Then I've got to feed the kids, do the laundry, take care of things there, too. You know how it is.

You: It's tiring just listening to you.

Janet: Sometimes I think I can't keep up with it. I know I'm falling behind here—closing files and such. I just hope I'm not messing up the claims, too.

You: Then you know you're behind on your closings.

Janet: Yes, but I don't think it's serious—yet.

You: What do you mean?

Janet: I don't think it's causing problems for the claimants or anyone. A couple of claimants flew off the handle about how long it was taking to process their claims, but I guess I'd be impatient, too, if I'd been flooded out of my home and lost everything.

You: So you're aware of the backlog you have but you don't think it's causing anyone else problems. The few complaints are from understandably impatient people.

Janet [*puzzled*]:   Is there something I ought to know?

You: I'm afraid so.

Janet [*defensive*]:   Why didn't someone say something?

You: Until now, no one has had any complaints. Your work has been very good, and I've shown my appreciation to you for that. But now they are complaining, and they've asked me to talk with you about it.

This week hasn't been easy for you, and it's been pretty hard on your claimants and on accounts payable, where they've been taking a lot of the heat you're not feeling. Some of those impatient claimants have been calling them instead of you, wanting to know where their checks are. Since Accounts Payable hasn't seen authorizations to pay, they refer back to you, but the people say they don't get any satisfaction from you.

Janet [*testy*]:   I don't know what they want from me.

You [*getting Janet to spell out the standards for herself*]:   You know the guidelines during this emergency, I'm sure.

Janet: Process every claim within two workdays of receipt of documentation. [*Adding quickly:*] But every file has so many claims, it's nearly impossible to close any file within two workdays.

You: Then, let's talk about what you can do to satisfy individual customer claims and keep them from calling Accounts Payable. That okay?

Janet [*somewhat dejected*]:   Sure, but we'd better look at what I've got to do, not just at what other people want.

You: That seems the place to start. Let's take a look at what you're doing.

Collaborating on Writing a Performance Appraisal—The Ideal Situation

Required annual formal reviews often receive a bad rap. But they do have a place in performance management—if they meet their own quality standards. An effective formal review reflects past experience and sets out a plan for continuous improvement and growth. Follow these guidelines for conducting performance appraisals that bring out the best in your employees:

1. Take a forward-looking orientation.
2. Anchor reviews on expectations (objectives and standards) created by the employee's job description.
3. Collaborate with the employee on writing the appraisal.
   a. Give the employee being reviewed an opportunity to

evaluate his own performance before the final version is written.

b. In a meeting, compare your review with hers. Discuss and resolve differences.

c. Discuss an overview of the whole review before getting into the details.

d. Discuss each dimension of the review (e.g., quality of work) separately.

e. Ideally, write the final review as a joint product.

4. Set aside ample time to hold a second meaning if your final review differs from what the two of you discussed previously.

5. When delivering a review to an employee with performance problems:

a. Point out the positive aspects of the performance before discussing the negatives.

b. Place negative feedback into an objective context (goals, objectives, and standards; previous discussions on the subject) and into a positive action plan for improvement in which both of you will play a part.

c. Recognize the other person's feelings, concerns, and problems.

d. Support the other person's self-esteem even as you discuss areas in which she needs to improve.

e. Let the other person identify the problems and their causes, even if that means giving you negative feedback about what you have or have not done.

f. Spell out the consequences of not improving performance during the next rating period, and the rewards for doing so.

g. Encourage the other person to solve her own problems.

6. Look to the future with growth and development plans.

Scenario—The Ideal Situation

Maria has had a few problems this past year. The new processing equipment seems to have her buffaloed. You have discussed this with her several times and spent a few extra hours on several occasions working on the math she has to learn to program the machinery properly. Both the quantity of work and its quality have suffered. Otherwise, Maria has done very well, contributing to the Quality Control team regularly and coming up with several important safety program suggestions. It's now annual review time, and you have to deal with the fact that Maria has these crucial problems that could hold her back.

Key Phrases
Setting Up a Review Session

"Let's go over the procedures."
"We can compare notes and settle disagreements."
"After we review . . . , we can discuss improvement or growth."

You: You know the procedures since we've done reviews several times before, but I always think it's best to go over them during every session, just to make sure we're on track with one another.

Maria: Sure, no problem. I've got my copy of the review here—worked on it over the weekend.

You: Good. We'll compare notes on them both, and if we disagree, we'll work through the disagreement and put the result into the final review. As usual, we'll start with your achievements, and then we can talk about areas in need of improvement.

Maria [*smiling*]: Let's cut through all that this time. I know I'm screwing up on my production and quality standards, so let's talk about that first.

Collaborating on Writing a Performance Appraisal—Surly Employee

Cooperative employees make it easier to give negative feedback in a review. On the other hand, resentful or resistant employees test your skills as well as your patience. Often, employees shift attention from their inadequate performance to other people, to the training, or to some other factor that they can't control. Your job, then, is to listen, to acknowledge any genuine external barriers to performance, and to help these employees focus on their responsibilities in the situation as well.

Scenario—Surly Employees

We all like to review the performance of the Maria of the first scenario. The surly Maria of the second scenario poses a different sort of problem.

Key Phrases
Keeping Focused

"What do you think is happening?"

"So, you think. . . ."

"I hear what you're saying, and. . . ."

"Let's take a look at what you are doing and how you are doing it."

"What can you do to. . . ?"

"What can I do to help you improve. . . ?"

You: You know the procedures, since we've done this several times before, but I always think it's best to go over them during every session, just to make sure we're on track with one another.

Maria [*a bit surly*]:   Sure. I've got a copy of the review here—worked on it over the weekend.

You: Good. We'll compare notes on them both and if we disagree—

Maria: And we probably will.

You: Oh? In what way?

Maria: You think the problems I'm having are my fault, but as I've told you before, that operator's manual isn't worth a damn, and I don't think you've explained the math very well. You've said it yourself—you have problems with some of that stuff.

You: So, you think that at least some of your problems stem from the manual and from my inability to explain it well enough.

Maria: Yep.

You: You're right. We do have a difference of opinion to work through before writing the final review. But, Maria, you've done a pretty good job overall, so why don't we do as we usually do: start with your achievements, then talk about areas in need of improvement.

Maria: Let's cut through all that. I know I'm screwing up on my production and quality standards, so let's just get down to it.

You: Okay. Tell me what you think is happening.

Maria: Like I've said before, the manual's written for college graduates, not for people like me. I just barely made it through high school. My math isn't up to the level the new processing equipment requires. When you hired me, we didn't need all that. This so-called reengineering program has put me behind an eight ball.

You: I hear what you're saying, yet I've also seen you improve in spite of your difficulties. What worked for you during this period?

Maria [*puzzled*]: What do you mean?

You: You're still not meeting expectations in quantity or quality of work, but you've moved up from some pretty bad figures in the beginning to a lot more respectable numbers. What did you do to move from where you were to where you are?

Maria: I studied the math. You know, you helped me, staying late a few days.

You: So, you studied the math. You took the math proficiency test in the manual a week ago and scored a 75. The first time you took the test, you scored a 48. That's a big jump.

Maria: Textbook stuff. Memorized it. But getting the formulas into the computer is another story.

You: Tell me about that.

Maria: Every time I have to change the mix, I have to put new formulas into the computer. That's when I go to pieces. You saw that yourself. I sometimes forget what formula to enter; other times I mess up the formula.

You: Scoring a 75 on a paper-and-pencil test is one part of it, but you still have problems executing the changes. Is that it?

Maria: You know it—and I don't think you're giving me enough help or time.

You: The standards are okay, then.

Maria: Oh, yeah. It's not the standards. It's the methods we have to learn to get there.

You: So, you see the problem is that I'm not giving you enough help or time to—to do what?

Maria: Here's what I wrote in my version of the review. I need more time to learn how to do the math, and I need more help from you to learn it.

You: Well, I agree that you need more time to learn the math, but what I wrote is that we should enroll you in a special class the manufacturer offers because I can't do more to help you than what I've already done. How do you feel about that?

Maria: On whose time and who'll pay for it?

You: It'll be on our time, and we'll pay for it.

Maria: I'll fall further behind.

You: You're in the hole already, and if you don't do this, you'll get in much deeper. Maria, you know your performance has already affected the level of your performance bonus. You won't get as much as you hope to get. You also know what'll happen if you don't bring your work up to standards within ninety days after this review: I'll have to put you on performance probation. Unless you improve your performance thirty days after that, I'll either have to transfer you to a lower-paying job—if one is available—or let you go. But if you get a handle on the stuff troubling you, you'll get your bonus—and you could even climb up the technical ladder to senior technician. That could mean a whole lot more money in every paycheck.

Maria: Yeah. I suppose you're right.

You: So, how do you think we should write this part of the appraisal?

Maria: Out of the 5 points, I guess I shouldn't get more than a 2, and then I'd say that I got a lot to learn still.

You: You're a lot harder on yourself than I am. I gave you 3 points because you've worked at it and you've shown a lot of improvement. I also said that the math's very difficult for you and that's where the problem is—but that you probably could correct it if you got help from the people who made the system. What do you think of that statement?

Maria: No quarrel with it.

You: Want to talk about this any more?

Maria: No. I think we've covered it all. Let's move on to the other categories.

Conclusion

Regularly conducted appraisals play an important role in managing performance and improving the quality of work. Every compliment for a job well done or criticism for a job poorly done—or not done at all—constitutes a performance review. Effective reviews begin before an employee begins work on the job; they begin when you develop or write a job description in which you set down the goals and objectives of the job and the standards by which success in the job will be measured. That job description forms the basis for monitoring performance, deciding whether the job is being done well or poorly, coaching or counseling to take corrective action, rewarding employees who do well, and disciplining or dismissing those who consistently fail to meet standards. The whole performance management system should be a continuous process rather than a once-a-year agony.

Chapter 8

Coaching To
Improve Performance

The quality and quantity of employee production reflect not only on the employees but also on their supervisors or managers. Therefore, coaching people for improving performance (upgrading their skills) and management go hand in hand. Coaching is important and requires:

- Giving feedback and identifying problems
- Solving problems
- Facilitating learning with regard to problem solving

When employees are not performing up to standard, one or more of the following conditions probably exists:

- They don't understand their jobs.
- They don't have the knowledge or the skills for doing their jobs well.
- They do not want to do their jobs.
- They have personal problems.
- They are unhappy with their work situation.
- They are unhappy with the quality of their supervision.
- They have not received proper or appropriate training.
- They have not been provided with proper and appropriate resources or equipment.
- They do not have a positive and productive environment in which to work.
- They do not receive proper and appropriate recognition for their efforts.

- They do not receive proper and appropriate rewards or compensation for their work.
- They do not receive proper and appropriate coaching and counseling from the people to whom they look for direction and guidance.

Proper and appropriate performance coaching or counseling provides the means for finding out which factors play what roles. The coach's most important role is to investigate the causes of the performance problem, and her most important skill is being a gatekeeper. Usually the solution presents itself when the cause is uncovered.

Missing the Mark—The Ideal Situation

A successful coach understands the following precepts:

- The failure to meet standards is an opportunity for creative problem solving.
- The beginning is always the most difficult stage of development.
- To give a person dignity is above all other things.
- Feelings are as important as facts.
- Mirroring bad feelings helps to lower the emotional temperature.

Scenario—The Ideal Situation

Polly has been working for you for a month, and her progress doesn't match the standards for other employees at this stage. She has a high school equivalency certificate and seems sufficiently literate to read and understand the training manuals. You have reviewed her training file and find nothing out of the ordinary. Now you must teach her how to fish (rather than *give* a fish to her).

Key Phrases
Coaching to Improve Performance

"The purpose of this meeting is to take a look at. . . ."
"I think you'll get a lot out of this meeting if. . . ."
"Let's look at the standards and how you're doing in relation to
    them."
"How do you feel about how you're doing?"
"What can you do to improve your performance?"
"What can the company or I do to help you?"

You [*beckoning to Polly, standing in the doorway of the office*]:   Come in. Close the door against the noise out there. Have a seat. [*You come out from behind the desk to sit next to the employee.*] How are you doing?

Polly: Fine. But I know I'm not meeting the production standards you set.

You: That's right. That's why we have these progress reviews. In fact, I'd like you to tell me what you think about your progress, and we can compare notes.

Polly: What I think?

You: Sure. You're the one doing the work, you chart your production daily. That's why I asked you to bring the charts with you.

Polly: I feel pretty bad. I'm afraid that if I don't improve, you're going to let me go.

You: So, you feel bad that you're not meeting the standard. It's not as if you don't care about it.

Polly: No. Not at all.

You: I've had employees who feel that the standards are too high for trainees.

Polly: I don't. I just wish I could meet them.

You: What do you think is holding you back?

Polly: I'm just not working fast enough, and I don't know how to get faster.

You: Let's talk about working faster. How many units are you turning out in an hour?

Polly: About three. The manual says I should practice five in an hour.

You: So, you're off standard by two units per hour. Every hour?

Polly: No. Sometimes I get five out the door.

You: What's different about the times when you do get them out the door?

Polly: I don't have to stop and redo anything.

You: Oh?

Polly: Yeah. I really want to get as many out of the door as I can, but I make mistakes, and then I have to stop and undo the mistakes. Here, look at this production record for yesterday. I even got seven finished each hour between nine and lunchtime. I didn't make any mistakes at all, but in the afternoon, I fell apart. I didn't finish five units during any hour of the afternoon.

You: What happened then?

Polly: I guess I felt rushed. Tired, too.

You: When do you make most of your mistakes?

Polly: Let's look at these production records a little closer. I guess the pattern's there, isn't it? I'm at my worst after lunch almost every day, when I'm tired and when I think I have to work faster to meet my daily quota.

You: So, you think the problem is a matter of trying to do too much too fast at the end of the day.

Polly: Mostly. You know, I really am a morning person. Always have been. That's probably all that's wrong.

You: Well, that could be a part of it. What do you think you can do about it?

Polly: Since I have to average five units an hour, I'll try to get out more units in the morning to make up for the slowdown in the afternoon. If I don't rush myself then, I won't tire so badly and make such terrible mistakes that I have to redo so often.

You: That could work in the short run but not in the long term. We need consistency of production, and letting yourself slow down in the afternoon will prevent consistency.

Polly: Oh?

You: I think we need to take a look at how you're assembling the units too. For now, I think we should work on quality, not quantity. You did that in the beginning. You were slow but sure. When the standard was only three units an hour, you did quite well each hour of the day. And although you got tired in the afternoon, too, you didn't have to redo anything. What do you think about what I just said?

Polly: Just being a morning person isn't the problem, I guess.

You: It may be part of it, but as you increased your speed, you began to fumble the connections you had to make in these units. [*Holding up a unit:*] Look at this one. You sent it out to the mounting unit yesterday *morning,* not yesterday afternoon. Look at these connections in here.

Polly: I missed that, didn't I?

You: Yes, you did. I think you need to slow down again. You'll fall behind for a short while perhaps, but you have to work on technique, on the fundamentals. Because you know you get tired after lunch, you speed up in the morning. You make more mistakes than you're aware of, and you tire yourself even more than you would get if you didn't try working so hard and so fast. What are you getting out of what I'm saying?

Polly: That I have to slow down the pace, especially in the morning. Conserve my strength and even out my performance. I'll make fewer mistakes and get more units finished that way.

You: That's right. When your technique is up to standard, your productivity will be also.

Polly: You'll give me the time?

You: You're still in your probationary period. Even though the manual says you should be producing five units an hour now, let's move it back to four. Slow down your fingers and let them learn the drill more efficiently before you speed them up again. When you come in, tomorrow I'll spend the first hour with you, to check what you're doing as you're doing it. If I see a mistake that you don't see, I'll call it to your attention and ask you to figure out how to correct it.

Polly: I don't know if I can do well with you standing over my shoulder.

You: I'll be there only to coach you. Then you can practice making the connections more efficiently for two days, and I'll check it again. If you can, we'll raise the bar. If not, we'll try the four per hour for another day. I think by the end of week you should be up to standard.

Polly: For this week, it's supposed to be six per hour.

You: I'm confident that by the end of the week, you'll be there. How do you feel about what we decided?

Polly: A *lot* better than when I came in. And, thanks. I really appreciate your help and your vote of confidence.

Missing the Mark—Defensive Employee

When dealing with a defensive employee, a successful coach knows know to encourage learning or a genuine commitment to making a change (as opposed to mere compliance). In this situation, the following tips will help:

- Lower the emotional temperature, and create a cool climate in which feelings are properly aired and managed.
- Give feedback.
- Mirror feelings.
- Paraphrase.
- Use pregnant silence to give the other person a chance to think and respond.

Scenario—Defensive Employee

Let's change the picture a little from the previous one. Pat was also hired four weeks ago, and her progress does not match the standards for other people at this stage. Like Polly, she has a high school equivalency certificate, so she should be sufficiently literate to read and understand the training manuals. You have reviewed her training file and find nothing out of the ordinary. The biggest difference from Polly is that Pat isn't cooperative.

Key Phrases
Coaching as Corrective Action

"There's no reason to be nervous about. . . ."
"We need to talk about how to improve. . . ."
"I'd like to hear your impressions of. . . ."
"The way I see it. . . ."

You [*beckoning to Pat, standing in the doorway of the office*]:   Come in. Close the door against the noise out there. Have a seat. [*You come out from behind your desk to sit next to the employee.*] How are you doing?

Pat: Fine. How are you?

You: I'm fine too. This is an awkward moment for both of us, isn't it? You and I both know that I want to talk about your progress during your first month.

Pat [*sullenly*]:   That's right.

You: Well, I don't want you to be nervous about it. This is a progress review, and we need to talk about a problem or two, but I promise that you'll walk out that door with all your body parts intact. In fact, I'd like you to tell me what you think about your progress, and we can compare notes.

Pat: What I think? What difference does that make?

You [*mirroring feelings detected in Pat's manner and tone of voice*]:   You seem angry about something.

Pat: Wouldn't you be, if you were in my shoes? I'm not meeting the standards.

You: That's why I'm asking how you feel about your progress.

Pat: I feel pretty bad. I'm afraid you're going to let me go during this probation period, and I need the job.

You: I know. [*Giving feedback to show you understand:*] So, you feel bad that you're not meeting the standard. It's not as if you don't care about it.

Pat: I care about it, but I also think that the standards are too high for trainees.

You: Oh? Tell me more.

Pat: What difference does it make?

You: Unless we get feedback from people, we don't know how to change what we're doing or improve on our procedures.

Pat: You'll just listen politely and then tell me to do what you pay me for or get out.

You [*mirroring*]: That's what you expect?

Pat: Yes.

You: Why do you feel that way?

Pat: You're the boss, aren't you? And the boss is always right—at least that's what I've always experienced in a job.

You: Sometimes the boss can make a mistake. But I can't know that I have unless I get feedback. Why do you think the standard's too high?

Pat: 'Cause I'm new on the job, and learning these new skills isn't as easy as it seems to you. You've been doing these things for years and years.

You [*laughing lightly*]: Well, I wouldn't say "years and years," but I've done them for a while. And, no, I don't think learning these skills is easy. Go on.

Pat: Maybe I need more training.

You: What do you mean? I need specifics. Didn't your training last long enough? Go into sufficient detail? Give you enough practice? Did I answer your questions when you didn't understand?

Pat [*softening and more relaxed; satisfied that she has been given a chance to talk and that she is being heard and understood*]: You were great. Really patient too. Maybe I could have used more practice before going out on to the floor. Maybe the training could have been a week longer to give more time to work on doing the job without sending the units into production. I'm working as fast as I can, and I don't know how to get faster.

You: Let's talk about working faster. How many units are you turning out in an hour?

Pat: About three. The manual says I should be doing five.

You: So you're off standard by two units per hour.

Pat: I guess so.

You: Every hour?

Pat: No. Sometimes I get five out the door.

You: What's different about those times when you do get them out the door?

Pat: I don't have to stop and redo anything.

You: Oh?

Pat: Yeah. I really want to get as many out the door as I can, but I make mistakes, and I have to stop and undo them.

You: So, the problem of quantity comes up when you make mistakes. If you don't make them, you meet the production standard right on.

Pat: Here—look at this production record for yesterday. I finished seven each hour between nine and lunchtime, and I didn't make any mistakes at all. But in the afternoon I fell apart. I didn't finish five units during any hour of the afternoon.

You: What happened then?

Pat: I guess I felt rushed. Tired, too. You're pushing me too hard.

You [*mirroring*]:   You're feeling pushed.

Pat: Yes. I think the numbers show it, too.

You: Okay. Let's look at those production records a little closer. When do you make most of your mistakes?

Pat: That's what I'm talking about. I'm at my worst after lunch almost every day, when I'm tired and when I think I have to work faster to meet my daily quota.

You: So, you think the problem's a matter of trying to do too much too fast at the end of the day.

Pat: Mostly. Maybe it's just because I'm really a morning person. Always have been. Maybe that's all that's wrong.

From this point, the conversation is the same as in the ideal situation because early in the dialog you lowered the emotional level Pat carried into the room and brought her to closure around the problem to solve: improving performance.

Conclusion

Successfully coaching an employee depends on your ability to manage the discussion—not on how well you can do the job yourself or how well you can give detailed instructions. You can offer your opinion, but you can't impose solutions. You can't give your employees the fish; you have to teach them how to fish for themselves. In this sense, coaching is really guiding: listening, probing, encouraging, exchanging information or opinions, resolving disagreements, and designing an action plan.

Chapter 9

Coaching for Growth And Development

Just as managers have to coach performance, they have to take responsibility for developing employees' skills and for the learning process. In other words, they have to coach their employees for growth and development.

Learning how to solve problems, to make decisions, and to help the business be successful goes beyond correcting job-related performance problems and contributes to employee growth. Sometimes, though, it's difficult for some supervisors to coach for growth. Maybe they worry about losing "good people, whom I've hired, trained, and sweated bullets to get up to speed." Maybe they don't see the growth of employees as a feather in their caps, partly because companies rarely reward them for growing employees. Yet if the company and its managers don't help employees continuously to improve skills, the company loses. In fact, helping employees upgrade quality, innovate or create new products, and provide exemplary customer service goes right to the bottom line and organizational survival itself.

Coaching for growth and development requires managers to expand as well. They need to:

- Increase their organizational knowledge about what and who gets things done.
- Get outside their own niche in the organization to develop networks of effective working relationships with other managers.
- Have an appreciation for continuous improvement.
- Feel a personal commitment to their own growth and development.

- Have an eye for talent and a willingness to encourage it.
- Feel a personal commitment to the growth and development of others.

Coaching for growth and development demands something of the company as well: career paths and career planning opportunities. Unless employees have somewhere to go in your company and have realistic expectations that they'll get there, their growth and development will benefit your competitors.

Coaching a Reluctant Employee

Coaching for growth usually requires that you trust people to do things they've never done before or do things they've had problems with in the past. It means encouraging them out of their comfort zones and beyond their current skill levels. Sometimes you may have to pull them kicking and screaming into open space. Following are a few ways that you can help employees grow on the job:

- Give employees opportunities to solve task-related problems and make decisions that affect what they do and how they do it.
- Solicit employees' opinions about work-related issues that affect them.
- Involve employees in planning and decision making for the work unit.
- Delegate meaningful extra work to employees. This is the meaning of job enrichment.

Scenario—Coaching a Reluctant Employee

Ralph does good work. Every project he does comes out looking better than expected and well ahead of schedule. You want to take advantage of his attention to detail by putting him in charge of a multifunctional team, but his reputation for rudeness and somewhat poor interpersonal relations precedes him.

Key Phrases
Coaching for Growth

"What do you think about. . . ?"

"How would you go about doing this?"

"Tell me the best way you see for. . . ."

"Here's the situation. . . . What do you think?"

"I'd like you to do something a little different from what you've been doing."

"I'd like you to take charge of. . . . How do you feel about the extra responsibility?"

"I need some help with this, and I think you can do it. How do you feel about that?"

"I think it's time for you to learn how to. . . ."

"How do you feel about taking on . . . ?"

"We're forming a task force, and I'd like to recommend you for it. How do you feel about that?"

You: Another successful project! Everyone downstream is crazy about the work you've done.

Ralph: Thanks, but it's no more than I expect.

You [smiling]: Yes. I suppose that's true. [*slight pause*] Ralph, I'd like to talk to you about another important project, one that involves leading a cross-functional team.

Ralph: You know you're buying trouble.

You: Your reason is . . . ?

Ralph: I usually don't get along well with other people on a job. I don't think I should do it.

You: Talk to me about what happens when you work in a team.

Ralph: You probably think I'm arrogant. Other people tell me I am. But when you hop around with turkeys, it's pretty hard to soar like an eagle. That's an old cliché, but it fits.

You: You think other people are turkeys.

Ralph: Most of them—present company excepted, of course.

You: Why exempt me?

Ralph [*laughing*]:   Because you're the boss?

You [*joining in the joke*]:   I'd hope for more than that!

Ralph: Well, yeah. You're sharp. You know what you're doing, and you know how to get the job done.

You: That's what's important to you: knowing what you're doing and knowing how to get the job done. Otherwise you're a turkey.

Ralph: Yeah. What else is more important?

You: Let me pose a problem to you, to see how you'd handle a situation. Let's say you're a manager, and you have a sharp employee who has run into a tough problem. What do you do?

Ralph: If he can't handle the job, find someone who can.

You: Remember, I said he's a sharp guy—does his job well, gets it done—but he's run into this one problem.

Ralph [*the light coming on quickly*]:   Help *him* solve it—don't do it *for* him.

You: Is he a turkey?

Ralph: Not if he's a sharp guy.

You: You have a problem working with other people. That make you a turkey?

Ralph: Naw. I know I've got this problem, but it doesn't affect how I do my job.

You: What makes a person a turkey?

Ralph: When they can't think for themselves. When the answer's staring them in the face and they can't see it. It seems to happen too often around here.

You: You see answers other people don't see, and you think they should see them, too.

Ralph: Sure. Look, I don't think I should head up that group. I get too impatient. I guess calling them turkeys really isn't fair, but sometimes I get frustrated when I'm working on something with others, and they don't know as much about their own tasks as I do. Or, when they get bogged down in trivia—or what seems like trivia to me. Who does what? Who gets credit for what? That sort of stuff.

You: One of the things about the team we're forming is that it's not only in your field of expertise—it's cross-functional. You'd be the only one with your specialized knowledge, and all the other people will be experts in their fields.

Ralph: Then why me?

You: Attention to detail. Problem-solving skills. A good sense of the task. But I am bothered by your people skills.

Ralph: Or lack of them. So, as I said, why me?

You: How do you feel about taking a leadership role?

Ralph: Hey! I'm an eagle, aren't I?

You: That means you'd like it?

Ralph: Sure, but I'm afraid it would have to be on my terms, and I don't think other people buy into my way of doing things.

You: Then you don't think you can pull it off?

Ralph [*after thinking about it*]:   I don't know. Okay, so everyone'll have their own expertise, but what about the trivia? It gets to me.

You: If you're going to soar like an eagle, Ralph, you'll have to learn how to manage "the trivia," as you call it. Those are process issues that go on in any and every group of people. All leaders have to learn how to come to grips with their own feelings about basic human needs—like inclusion and recognition—who does what and who gets credit for what.

Ralph: You think I can handle it?

You: I asked you to do this because I think you can learn how to do it. I think you can turn into one fine team leader, and we need people with your task-oriented skills, even though we have to bring you up to speed with your people skills.

Ralph: I don't know. I'd need help.

You: So does everyone else, at one time or another.

Ralph: Okay. If you think I can do it, and you want me to, I'll do it. You'll help me learn how to run a work group and not run over it, won't you?

You: Only if you need the help—and only if you take responsibility for rising to the challenge. If the project team falls apart from your lack of leadership, you can't shift the blame on to me.

Ralph: Hey! I need help from the start. Will the group accept me? My reputation is pretty bad.

You: We're putting the whole group through a week-long, intensive team-building exercise beginning Monday, and I'll give you some additional guidance for how to get past your reputation. Then it's up to you to prove to them that you can lead and not bully.

Getting to Know Your Employees—The Ideal Situation, Part 1

Coaching for development picks up where coaching for growth leaves off. As a person grows, she has to see where that growth is leading her. Otherwise why would she bother to grow?

Reluctance to fraternize with employees makes it difficult for managers to get to know the people reporting to them. Spending a few social minutes over a cup of coffee is called a "waste of time." To some managers, having lunch with subordinates rather than with peers seems "beneath" them. Yet getting the best from other people is part of a manager's job, and you can't get the best from them unless you know what will reinforce the best that they can give. To uncover what those reinforcers are:

1. Find out what you can about your employee's interests, needs, and aspirations.
2. If possible, talk about the employee's interests, skills, and values in a nonthreatening environment and at a neutral time (*not* during a performance appraisal session).

Scenario—The Ideal Situation

Cynthia, a new employee whose education and background lend themselves to several different areas in the company, seems to be eager to advance into management. She talked about her ambitions during her hiring interview; now a lunchtime conversation with her gives you a chance to find out more about her.

Key Phrases
Coaching for Development

"How do you feel about working here?"

"Let's talk about what you'd like to do with your career."

"What would you like to be doing five years from now?"

"If you could choose any position in this company, which would it be?"

"What do you want to get out of your work here?"

"Your interests, skills, and values—how could you best satisfy them here?"

"What kind of work do we have here that fits with your interests, skills, and values?"

You: You've been with us now for six months. We're always looking for ways to improve how we treat employees. We can't get much from unhappy employees, and we know it. I'd like to ask a direct and honest question about how you like working for us, and I'd like a direct and honest answer. Okay?

Cynthia [*puzzled*]: Sure.

You: What do you think of our company as a place to work?

Cynthia: That is direct and honest! I'm just glad I can say I like it. What if I didn't like it here? Could I have told you?

You: Yes, because that's how *we* grow. What are some of the things you like?

Cynthia: The openness we have right now, for one thing. The friendliness. The teamwork. The pay and benefits are good, too. But the opportunities for advancement—that's the most important thing.

You: How so?

Cynthia: I'd like to move up into management. I worked hard for my bachelor's, and I'll probably do the weekend graduate program at the university for my master's.

You: If you could have any one position in this company, what would it be?

Cynthia: You probably expect me to say CEO, right?

You: Why not?

Cynthia: I don't know if that's what I really want. It seems more like a political job to me. To tell you the truth, I'm not sure I know enough about management positions here to know which I'd like most. I'd like to stay in my field if I could, but that's a pretty narrow path, and it seems somewhat crowded right now.

You: Let's talk about other interests. What sorts of things do you like to do?

Cynthia: Outside of work, I like sailing best, but I doubt if we have a vice presidency of sailing.

But I know what you mean. My job's pretty technical—I'm even called a nerd by some of own friends—but I'm not just a technical person. I like talking with people, working with them, helping them. I don't know that there's anything around here for that.

You: Possibly there is, but what do you mean when you say, "I like talking with people"?

Cynthia: I once thought about being a schoolteacher. I think kids ought to learn my job's basic skills in high school, but I don't think I'm cut out for teaching at that level. Now what did you mean by "possibly there is"?

You: I work closely with Human Resources—not just because it's part of my job but because I think they make an important contribution to the company. You remember I told you during the orientation that we have a career planning unit in Human Resources. You might want to talk with them at some point soon. But tell me more about your interest in teaching.

Cynthia: When I was a senior in college, I had an opportunity to teach some lower-level classes because my professor was out for two weeks. That was great for me.

You: That was quite an honor. But, then, I know you're good; that's why we hired you. So how did that go?

Cynthia: Great! Out of forty students, only one person, darn him, flunked the test my prof gave them when she got back. She was great, too. You remember, she was one of my references.

You: Yes, I remember. So you really enjoyed teaching adults, and you did it well enough for almost everyone to pass the test. What area are you going to concentrate in when you go to graduate school?

Cynthia: I don't know. Maybe more advanced studies in what I do best. I'll tell you, though, I'm afraid I'll put myself into a dead end if I do that.

You: Maybe I can help. Here are a few exercises I think you could do to get a handle on what you want to do. The first one is called a SWOT analysis, from the first letter of the important word in four questions:
1. What are my **S**trengths?
2. What are my **W**eaknesses?
3. What are my **O**pportunities?
4. What are the **T**hreats to me and mine?

Then ask yourself three more questions:

1. What can I do?
2. What do I want to do?
3. What's available to me?

Use these questions to draw a Venn diagram, like this:

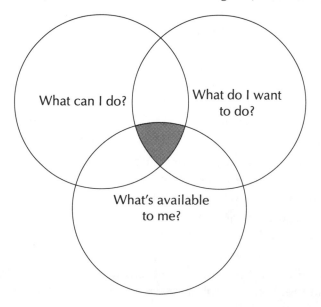

Now, where the three circles overlap, that seems like a good bet for you to pursue.

Getting to Know Your Employees—The Ideal Situation, Part 2

Once you get an employee tuned into the process of looking ahead, you have to follow through:

1. Know how to direct the employee's interests, needs, and aspirations into avenues needed by the business.
2. Provide information about how to go about finding ways to prepare for future opportunities.

Scenario—The Ideal Situation, Part 2

Cynthia warms up to the process and comes back with some new ideas for her future development.

Cynthia: I've done the SWOT exercises and Venn diagram, and I think I know how to use my technical expertise and satisfy my urge to teach.

You: What are you considering?

Cynthia: Training. Technical training. But I don't know how that'll work here.

You: It will satisfy your interest in working with other people. You know we like to grow our own here, and that's why we have the career development center in Human Resources. You should talk with them soon. They can also tell you more about the training division at Corporate than I can, but I do know that they often have a need for tech trainers, and you might qualify for that someday. It's also a road into a larger Human Resources role at Corporate. What do you think of that possibility?

Cynthia: That sounds interesting. What more can you tell me?

You: It's a lot like what you said about teaching those college classes. Adults. Skills you have and can teach. Immediate application on the job. Technical training makes an immediate impression on bottom-line figures.

Cynthia: How about management? I really would like to get into management.

You: From what I know—and you'll have to check this out—the career path leads from training coordinator to supervisor to manager to director. And it could lead into other Human Resources jobs. It depends a lot on what you study for your master's.

Cynthia: What do you mean?

You: If you want to get into management, technical skills won't be enough. We recognize technical competency with senior technician ranks, but managers need other skills unrelated to technical competency. We don't practice the Peter principle here, so we don't promote people into roles they're not suited or prepared for. You might consider an M.B.A. or a degree in human resources management—that sort of thing. Human Resources has many roles here. Even though we downsized that function last year, the need for regional or corporate Human Resources people still exists.

Cynthia: That does sound interesting. And I appreciate what you said about preparing myself for management. I guess I'm like everyone else—figure if you're good at what you do, you'll get promoted to manage it.

You: Some places, yes, but not here. We know that a lot of people have trouble making the transition. That's why we encourage them to take human relations and management courses. Corporate has a good management development program, and you need to look at some of the premanagement skills programs offered.

Conclusion

Organizations trying to develop a continuous learning-as-you-do environment ask managers to lead the process. Managers lead by example when they buy into continuous learning; their growth encourages everyone to emulate them. At the same time, everyone needs mentors, peers, or people at higher levels in the organization. In fact, in a genuine learning organization, the learning begins at the top and flows throughout the ranks.

The two ways in which you can coach for growth and development weave together into a coherent pattern. Giving people opportunities to solve problems, make decisions, and enter into goal setting and planning helps them take on more and more responsibility for themselves and for the business. This leads to developing their readiness to move forward into senior technical levels or into management. At this point, managers need to turn to other ways of handling their employees: listening to people talk about themselves; inquiring into their interests, skills, and values; pointing out paths they might take; helping them find the right path for them. Even if the organization doesn't reward you specifically for this coaching, you will have the satisfaction of watching your employees find themselves and their way into the future.

Section IV
Managing Relationships

Unless we are hermits, we come into contact with people from different backgrounds and life experiences that race, gender, age, or disability have affected and influenced. From time to time, we come into nose-to-nose conflict with other people, and we have to deal with them because we have no alternative.

In my research and experience, I've found that a good many work-related, stress-induced illnesses originate in difficulties that exist between people on the job. An environment can be hostile to anyone who feels demeaned or belittled and harassed. It can also be hostile to anyone feeling anger, resentment, and frustration in a difficult work situation.

This section is about coping with a hostile environment, regardless of what produces it. Communicating with difficult people, managing differences, managing conflicts, and building relationships with other people all require candid approaches in which what you say or do changes a negative experience to a positive one—or at least one in which you and the other person can live and work without rancor and distaste.

For anything I suggest in these chapters to work, certain assumptions have to hold true:

- Everyone in a conflict has an interest to satisfy and, usually, a position to support.
- Personal interests and positions often create attitudes that are difficult to influence.
- You and the other person want to change a negative experience to a positive one.
- You and the other person have an opportunity to make the change.
- Left to itself, the situation can produce negative consequences for either one or the other of you or for the workplace itself.
- Working together to resolve the relationship will have positive consequences and is worth the effort.

The last assumption is extremely important, because it dictates whether you should do something about the situation. If the benefits of confronting the other person and taking concerted action don't outweigh the liabilities, telling the other person what is on your mind may make a bad situation worse. Or, speaking your piece and letting it go at that may be the best you can gain from the fray. Nevertheless, before you give up on someone or something, consider the consequences of doing nothing at all.

All of the dialogs in this book include questioning techniques, but none are more specific or directed than the questions used while interviewing people during an investigation of charges of harassment, and no others raise more red flags to which managers need to pay particular attention. Many questions or comments, even nonverbal gestures, during an investigation can be out of line or slanted. At the same time, careful investigation is mandated, and quick corrective action, including firing a harasser, is needed if the allegations are true or reasonable.

Chapter 10

Communicating With Difficult People

What's a difficult person? Someone who chews gum noisily? Takes your existence for granted? Refuses to do extra work? Comes in late and leaves early? None of those are what I mean by *difficult*. Annoying, maybe, but not someone whose behavior regularly interferes with your ability to get along with him and/or to get your work done effectively or on time. He seems to be completely unmanageable and seems to take perverse pleasure in *not* getting along. And it's someone you have to work with regularly or otherwise can't avoid: a peer, an employee reporting to you, your boss. Communicating with the other person seems impossible to you when you believe you are willing to yield, or to accept feedback, or to confront issues, but he is *unwilling*.

People can be difficult in one of two ways:

1. Impossible or difficult *to you*. Only you feel a real need for creating change.
2. *Most of the people around them* find them impossible or difficult, and everyone affected feels a need for change.

When talking about difficult people, we're tempted to label them with words like *aggressive* or *passive*. Rather, avoid labeling people or calling them names; doing so only aggravates the problem. I prefer to talk only about *behavior* and how to respond to it. People can change what they do, not who they are.

When people protect their interests by adopting rigid positions, they escalate conflicts. Therefore, it's important for people to recognize they can satisfy their interests more effectively if they develop flexible positions.

There is more than one way to meet a need or wish. At the same time, you're the only person whose interests and positions you can control. So when asking that other people change their habits (often deep-seated ones), you must be willing to expect no more from them than you expect from yourself: a willingness to try to change a pattern of their behavior that comes in conflict with your needs, wishes, wants, or requirements. If you're the boss, they may be willing to comply with a demand, but compliance is not genuine commitment. Only if they can see that you want to deal with the situation in an atmosphere of mutual respect and friendship will you get them to listen.

Keep the following points in mind when dealing with someone you consider difficult:

- Something you say or do could trigger the behavior that annoys you the most.
- Chances are he doesn't realize that he is riling you or that you're upset with him.
- Different difficult people may provoke you in different ways: demanding attention by overwhelming others; holding back anger and keeping to himself, never really telling you what he thinks or feels; talking endlessly about what to you seems irrelevant trivia; carrying the burdens of the world on his shoulders, rarely smiling, rarely being pleasant; or manipulating everyone.
- Sometimes the climate or limited resources where you work calls out the worst in all of us.

So how do you handle all these people? The general guidelines set out below give you some idea of what to do or say, and the dialogs that follow will show you how to be assertive without being aggressive, how to solicit support for change, and how to plan and implement an action plan for change.

Communicating with Someone Who Claims To Know Everything

When communicating with difficult people, follow these guidelines:

- Look to yourself first. Are you doing anything to evoke the behaviors that annoy you the most? Are you reacting badly or overreacting to what the other person is doing?
- Separate the behavior from the person, and deal with that. Recognize that the difficulty is in the relationship, not necessarily in the person; it's a matter of how you and she perceive one another and how much tolerance you have for each other's behavior.
- Look for special circumstances that produce special behaviors (e.g., work or career frustrations, financial problems, a sick child, or unemployed spouse). Are you managing your reactions to uncommon or transient behavior?
- Accept one another as you are and for what you are.
- Help the other person see for herself the problem in the relationship; self-discovery leads to genuine change.
- Act assertively, expressing your feelings and beliefs without hostility or other forms of aggression.
- Ask for support for creating a positive change in the relationship.
- Plan the change and implement it, rather than let "things take care of themselves."
- Identify organizational factors that may contribute to the behavior. You may not be able to change the organizational factors, but you and the other person need to understand them in order to manage your reactions to them. If you do own some power to influence the climate, encourage changes in the situation.

Scenario—Someone Who Claims to Know Everything

Tony, a recent Ph.D. recipient in his first job as an assistant professor of education, irritates everyone, including the chairperson of the department (you). He minored in philosophy and considers himself to be an expert in educational philosophy and psychology. During his first semester, he became very disturbed over how some of the education students misstated or oversimplified various philosophical theories of knowledge and learning. After finding out that they had all taken a philosophy of education course from an associate professor, he decided to confront the older man. In a rage, the older teacher unloads on you and demands an apology and that the "young whipper snapper learn his place."

Key Phrases
Communicating with Someone Who Knows It All

"That's an interesting perspective."
"What do you think of . . . ?"
"When you talk like that, I get upset because. . . ."
"Other people have told me their feelings, and I agree that. . . ."
"How do you feel about these alternatives?"
"I'd like you to consider these alternatives."
"I'd like your help resolving. . . ."

You [*after exchanging pleasantries*]:   Professor Allen visited today. He was more than mildly upset.

Tony: *He* was upset! Do you know what he's teaching our students? He's got it all wrong! Even when he's right, he oversimplifies things to the point that people are walking around with empty concepts.

You: You seem convinced he's wrong.

Tony: Test papers from students who take his course show he's wrong. If all of them hadn't been wrong or oversimplifying what their sources said, I would've said it was them, not him.

You: How many is "all of them?'

Tony: Two-thirds of the people in my class have been through his.

You: Okay. For the sake of argument, let's say they're repeating what Dr. Allen taught them. How do you think you handled this situation?

Tony: What do you mean?

You: I'd like your help to resolve this situation.

Tony: Okay.

You: When you spoke with him, what did you say, and how did you say it?

Tony: I told him what the students said, told him that my degree includes a minor in philosophy, and showed him where he had misled them—that he was wrong on some points and that on others he oversimplifies.

You: The other day, when you and I disagreed, you told me I was wrong, too. How do you think I felt about that?

Tony: You laughed and passed it off, so I guess you were okay with it.

You: I seemed okay with it because I know you better than Dr. Allen does, and we've established a relationship. Still, I didn't appreciate your choice of words. Other people, Dr. Allen being just one of several who have complained, appreciate your candor much less than I do. Are you willing to talk about this, look at some alternative ways of talking with people, and making some changes?

Tony [*testily*]: That's dishonest! If they don't like what I have to say, they can talk with me about it. When I think they're wrong, why shouldn't I tell them what I think—straight out? Bluntly. Honestly.

You: You think that blunt honesty is the best policy.

Tony: I know this subject better than anyone else in the department. Why shouldn't I correct people when they're wrong? They can do the same to me. I won't get upset.

You [*smiling*]: How do you feel right now?

Tony [*puzzled*]: How do *I* feel? I'm not upset with you. I'm upset with people complaining about me behind my back. What are they saying that they can't say to my face?

You: With blunt honesty?

Tony: Sure.

You [*still calm and pleasant*]: I've heard words like *know-it-all, pain in the tookis, busybody, unpleasant, rude.* My own description is more charitable: *young, naive,* and *foolish.* Those enough blunt, honest names for your behavior since you've been here?

Tony [*shaking his head*]: I guess people don't accept me as I am, that's all.

You: What do you want them to do?

Tony: Just accept me as I am.

You: Since we feel you're trying to change us and are pushing us around in the process, are you willing to do the same for us: accept us as we are?

Tony [*after a pregnant silence*]: I'm blowing it, aren't I? I guess maybe we should talk about it. Try to undo the damage.

You: I don't know that you can, but it's worth a try, at least for me. I like you. You're bright. You have creative ideas that the department needs. All reasons why I encouraged the search committee to hire you, but I'd like you to consider alternative methods of talking with other people. You'll get along better, and people will listen to your expertise rather than reject what you have to say, whether or not you're right.

Tony: Sounds as if it's something I'd better do.

Communicating with Someone Who Doesn't Speak Up

People who don't talk much or who timidly express themselves pose different challenges. To get them to open up, do the following:

- Create a safe, secure climate.
- Give appropriate feedback and be an encourager (using many open-ended gatekeepers).
- Listen, and let the other person know you're listening.
- Encourage the other person to explore the problems she creates by her behavior.

Scenario—Someone Who Doesn't Speak Up

Allison rarely talks under any circumstances. She does her job and stays clear of other people. In group meetings, she sits apart and contributes only when specifically asked, but she knows a lot and has good ideas. On several occasions, when working closely with you on some project or other, she seemed more reticent, more withdrawn. She seems angry—arms folded across her chest, chair pulled away, back rigid—but she hasn't said anything about it. Since you and Allison are peers, you want her to be open, but you don't understand what's wrong.

Key Phrases
Breaking the Silence Barrier

"I really do want to know what you're [thinking/feeling]."

"What do you [think/feel] about. . . ?"

"When you don't say anything, I [don't know/believe/conclude/ feel]. . . ."

"We can't resolve difficulties between us unless you speak up."

"We need your contribution in order to. . . ."

"Your participation is important to us."

You [*after your work together is finished*]:   Do you have a few minutes? I'd like to talk with you a bit—a personal matter.

Allison: Okay, but only a few minutes.

You: Then I'll get to the point. It seems to me, when we're working together, that you're angry with me or don't like me—or something. I'd like us to talk about what I'm feeling. If I'm wrong, I want to correct my thinking, and if I'm right, I want to correct what's wrong between us. We have to work together often, and I'd rather we did it on friendly terms. How do you feel about this?

Allison: Okay.

You: Then I'd really appreciate some feedback about how you see me and feel about me. [*After a pregnant silence:*] At the least, I'd like to know if my perceptions are accurate or fair.

Allison [*sighing, reluctant*]:   This is very hard for me—talking about my feelings. [*After waiting a bit:*] You understand that?

You: Yes, I do. What reassurances do you need that'll encourage you to speak openly with me?

Allison: I hate confrontation.

You: You expect me to get angry or upset?

Allison: I think you will.

You [*laughing lightly*]:   I might get more upset if I don't know what's wrong. Please, I want to hear what you say, and regardless of what you say, I'll keep the peace. If I don't, you can end the conversation on the spot.

Allison [*after a pregnant silence; hesitant at first*]:   I—I don't—you're right, I don't like you. I find you domineering, too bright for your own good. You usually seem to know what I'm going to say before I say it. You even finish my sentences. That gets me mad.

You: You feel I create barriers for you.

Allison: Sometimes a wall.

You: How do I do that and when?

Allison: I'm really uncomfortable with this.

You: Please, Allison. This is important to me, and I think it'll do us both good.

Allison: All right, but I don't think you'll like this. [*After thinking about it a moment:*] I'll tell you something, and most of the time you'll answer, "I know," or, "That's what I say," or, "I agree." At times you say something like that and immediately move to something else, as if what I said was unimportant.

You: So, if I understand you, you feel I actually prevent you from talking.

Allison: Not entirely. I'm basically shy to begin with, so I don't talk a lot. That's why, I guess, I feel put down when I talk with you. That's what's most important: I feel put down.

You: What can I do to change things?

Allison: Listen to me, the way you're listening now. No comments. No can-you-top-this. I think I've said more to you in the last two minutes than I have in the last two weeks.

You: I'll make myself more aware of saying those things. I'll make a real effort to listen to you this way, but I need two things from you, too.

Allison: What's that?

You: Feedback when you feel that I'm running over you and a greater effort to contribute when we're together. Your participation and contribution are very important—not only to me but to the whole group.

Allison: I don't like confrontation.

You: A signal, that's all I'll need. Put your finger to your lips. Shake your head. Blink twice. Please. I need your help if you want me to tear down that wall. A plan for change. That's what I'm asking for.

Allison: I guess I can do that. Then maybe I'll feel more comfortable talking in the group too.

Conclusion

Communicating with difficult people is never easy. Truly difficult people usually don't pay much attention to their own behavior, and often they don't pay much attention to how other people feel about them. But, you must deal with them. In the rest of the chapters in this section, we'll examine some of the conditions that make it seem as if the other person is difficult when in reality the problems lie in different perspectives, different values, different cultures, or different life experiences. The guidelines set out at the beginning of this chapter can help get you through some of the other situations as well.

Chapter 11
Managing Differences

Difficult situations sometimes imply difficult people but not always. Judgmental behavior usually implies differences of beliefs or values, but that doesn't make the other person difficult as I defined it in the previous chapter. Opinions, beliefs, and values vary from person to person, and often not on the basis of facts. Often, what we call "facts" derive from a bias or preconceived notion, and those judgments create barriers between people. The same holds true for differences that arise from cultural diversity or life experiences. Under most circumstances, you manage the differences between you by exploring how the two of you can resolve your differences, or at least accommodate them.

Gaps between what people intend to communicate and the effect they have on other people come from a variety of sources:

- Personal experiences and history
- Expectations, beliefs, values, and attitudes from one's culture of origin, acquired mainly from family
- Language (acquired mainly from your culture of origin)
- Expectations, beliefs, values, and attitudes from one's acquired culture, acquired mainly from secondary associations (e.g., education and profession)

Managing Differences of Beliefs And Values—Talking with a Judgmental Person

Your way of looking at the world may not be the only "right" way. Your interpretations of words may not be the only way to think about things. Your solutions to problems may not be the only alternatives for solving them. The fresh views of situations brought by people from diverse backgrounds and with diverse opinions, beliefs, and values can enrich everyone's life and promote innovation in business, but they can also erect barriers to effective working relations. You need to recognize, examine, and overcome these barriers in order to facilitate communication, to organize experience productively, and to prevent them from undermining your efforts. Managing differences of beliefs and values begins with these principles:

- Recognize everyone's right to his own opinions, beliefs, values, or feelings.
- Learn from differences; use diversity to help solve problems and make decisions, while being alert to the possibility that those differences can interfere with work relationships.
- When another person expresses opinions, beliefs, values, or feelings in a nonproductive manner, help him see that what he is doing comes between you.
- Be forthcoming and assert your opinions, beliefs, or feelings in a friendly, constructive manner.
- Seek an amicable resolution.

Scenario—Talking with a Judgmental Person

Frank has been with the company "forever," people say. Those who know him best tolerate his idiosyncrasies, one of which is that he is a confirmed astrology buff—not the newspaper kind, but the very serious charting-and-religious-fervor kind. One of the first questions he asks anyone he meets is, "What's your sign?" Sometimes he doesn't bother with the formalities but blurts out, "You're a Scorpio. I can tell by the way you talk." When he's right, he crows; when he's not, he finds some way of slipping out of the error. "On what day were you born, and at what time?" When you tell him, he'll say something like, "Well, that explains why I missed your sign," and you have no idea what he means. Newer employees find him unbearable, and so do you. Right in the middle of a meeting with you and Doreen, Frank started to argue in a manner no one else could follow.

Key Phrases
Probing for Differences

"What do you mean by that?"

"What makes this important to you?"

"Let's talk about how we see things and what we do with the data."

"We both have to want to accommodate one another, or we will. . . ."

"What do you want to get out of this working relationship?"

"This is what I want to get out of this working relationship."

"How can we resolve the differences or at least arrive at a détente?"

Frank: You know, I don't think you and I can ever agree on anything.

You: Why do you say that?

Frank: I don't think this is the place to discuss it.

You: You brought it up.

Doreen: Look. I think this meeting's over, so I'll just get out of the way.

Frank: No. Don't go.

You: I think we need to talk this out, and maybe it's a good idea if we do adjourn this meeting and let Doreen get back to her work.

Frank [*after Doreen leaves*]: I don't think you needed to talk to Doreen that way.

You: How did I talk to her?

Frank: You just dismissed her.

You: You raised an issue between us, Doreen volunteered to leave, and I think we need to hash it out before it gets out of hand. Why do you think we're at a standoff?

Frank: You're a Pisces, and I'm a Gemini. We're a bad mix.

You: What does that mean?

Frank: We see things differently, we want different things, and we go about getting them in different ways.

You: That's true of almost everyone, so what difference do our signs make?

Frank: A lot of difference.

You: I truly don't understand this. Why is the difference in our signs important to you?

Frank: Let's see if I can explain this in a way you can understand. Two people born under antagonistic signs shouldn't marry or work together. They come at the world from diametrically opposed perspectives and values—as we do.

You: You believe this.

Frank: Profoundly.

You: Frank, I'm going to tell you what I think and feel, and I'd like us to reach an accommodation, just so we can work together and use these disagreements in a constructive way. Is that okay?

Frank: Whatever you want.

You: Frank, you have to want it, too, or it won't work. If you really want this conversation, I'd like you to tell me what you want out of it.

Frank: I think we don't talk at the same level about the same things. I see things from my perspective; you see things from yours. Our stars are in a bad combination.

You: What's wrong with having two different perspectives looking at the same point?

Frank: I can't come together with you. You're a Pisces—the sensitive, creative kind, born at the end of February. I'm a Gemini, born in the middle of June. I'm tougher minded and clearer headed than you are. I see the differences, and I'm adjusting for them, but you don't see the differences and can't make the adjustment.

You: I have trouble with your analysis, and I'm teed off by all this. I think I see some preconceptions that have nothing to do with you or me as people. You see our differences as written in the stars, and what's written in the stars will be.

Frank: That's what I mean. You don't respect me for my views on astrology, and it creeps into everything we do.

You: That's what you see as our differences. Do you want to add anything to that?

Frank: No. There's nothing else we need to say.

You: Frank, to be honest, I don't care what you believe about astrology. To me it's like religion. If yours works for you, believe in it. On the other hand, I do care when you judge everything I say as "just another soft-minded Pisces idea." And that's how you come across to me. I can't know what I'm talking about because I'm a Pisces.

Frank [*after a pregnant silence*]:   You want me to respond to that?

You: Yes.

Frank: I'm a Methodist. Astrology's a hobby, not my religion.

You: Please stick to the issue, which I see as you judging everything I say—or most things—as soft-minded Pisces nonsense. I'd like you to stop judging my ideas long enough to listen to them and then shoot them down on their merits, not on some preconceived notion of what my ideas are like.

Frank: I don't do that.

You: That's how it seems to me. What do you say we work out an agreement here—that we talk with each other about business issues in a businesslike way, without invoking the stars or anything other than the data and sound logic. How about it?

Frank: What do you want me to do?

You: Listen to me. Look at the data when we disagree. Talk only about the business issues in front of us.

Frank: But if I think conditions aren't favorable, why should I agree with you?

You: Let consensus rule, not the stars. If I'm later proved wrong, tell me I told you so. That's okay with me. We're not really solving our problem, but we'll at least be able to work together.

Frank [*with a set jaw*]:   What do I get out of this? You're asking me to suppress my opinions. Why should I?

You: I'm not asking you to suppress anything. Tell me what you

think; that's okay. But let's not make your astrological opinions
the final judge of my ideas or action plans. That's all I ask.

Frank: And you won't ridicule my beliefs?

You: If you think I do that, I'll be sure to watch myself in the future.

Confronting a Potentially Hostile Situation—The Ideal Situation

People's experiences shape their perceptions and their values. With
more and more racial and ethnic minorities, women, older people,
and people with disabilities entering the mainstream of the workforce, learning how to deal with those differences becomes very
important. These guidelines will help when you work with a diverse group of employees:

- See people as individuals, not as representatives of a group.
- View differences of perceptions or values as opportunities
  for sharing, learning, and creativity.
- When you believe that someone is mistreating or even harassing you as a result of some characteristic differences,
  confront that person immediately and report the problem to
  someone in authority.
- Air the differences between you and the person you believe
  is causing you discomfort in an attempt to prevent repeated
  incidents.
- Reach an agreement regarding how each of you will treat
  the other in the future.

Scenario—The Ideal Situation

Ron grew up in the backwoods of West Virginia. After serving three
years in the army, rising to the rank of sergeant, he moved to the city,
where he took a job on a loading dock at a factory. Intelligent and
quick witted, trained to be and experienced as a leader, he soon
found himself promoted to shipping dock supervisor. After going to a
special training program on tariffs and transportation, he was promoted to shipping manager. Ron reports to you, a Jew. Ron has had

little experience with Jews. He heard all kinds of stories about Jews as he was growing up, particularly from his father—that they were greedy, sneaky, and rich. And he fervently believes that the Jews killed Jesus. He met a few Jews in the army, but he had little to do with them and never had to take orders from one. Now he has to talk with one every day.

Key Phrases
Responding to Unkind Remarks

"What you said [bothers/offends] me."
"Please don't say things like that to me or in front of me."
"I'd rather you didn't say. . . ."
"What does that mean to you? . . . Here's what it means to me."

You: Ron, I was just looking over these invoices, and I found this one from Ace Trucking. That's the lowest rate we've ever gotten from them. Good work.

Ron: Well, I Jewed 'em down good.

You: Excuse me?

Ron: They came in on a real high bid, but they're the best in the area, and I thought we should use 'em, so I Jewed 'em down.

You: Ron, I'm going to ask you not to use that expression, at least not around me.

Ron [*puzzled*]: What expression? I don't understand you.

You: "Jewed 'em down." That's offensive to me.

Ron [*trying to laugh it off*]: Oh, it's just a way of talking. That doesn't mean anything to me.

You: But it means something to me, and I find it very offensive.

Ron: Gosh. I didn't mean to offend you, and I really don't know how I did it.

You: What does "Jew 'em down" mean to you?

Ron: It means "get the best price."

You: Then why not say that instead?

Ron: I guess I can, but what's wrong with the other way?

You: It originally meant to take unfair advantage of someone in ne-
gotiating a price; it reflects the belief by non-Jews that Jews engage in unfair business practices. That's the meaning that has
stuck with the Jewish people I know, and we find the phrase
offensive.

Ron: I'm truly sorry. I won't use it again.

You: Thanks, I appreciate that.

Managing Deliberate Discrimination Or Harassment—Talking With A Close-Minded Person

You need to confront deliberate harassment that comes from nar-
row-mindedness even more directly and emphatically than you do
the sort of well-meaning but misguided misadventures (such as the
one in the previous dialog). Whether we're talking about racial or
ethnic discrimination or harassment, sexual harassment, religious
harassment, or another specific kind of harassment, the operative
noun is *harassment*. The only way to stop it is to confront it:

1. Identify the specific acts or words to which you object, and
   carefully document your objections.
2. Explain why you object. Don't be intimidated by a person's
   status.
3. Explain the steps you intend to take if the behavior doesn't
   stop.
4. Explain the consequences if the behavior doesn't stop.
5. Explain the positive aspects of overturning the negative situation.

Scenario—Talking with a Close-Minded Person

Edith has been vice president of sales at Midwest Radio and TV Com-
munications for less than two months, and she has already made her
feelings very well known. Only thirty-four years old and ambitious,

she has told the whole sales staff that she's on a youth movement: hire only recent college graduates to get new blood into the organization. When the sales manager in the eastern region quit to take a promotion with a competitor, she promptly replaced him with a former college classmate, a man who had been with the company less than a year. You, fifty-two years old, with twenty years of radio and television time sales and sales management, feel passed over unfairly.

Key Phrases
Confronting Someone You Believe Has Treated You Unfairly or Illegally

"I believe I've been treated unfairly or illegally."
"I'd like an explanation of. . . . "
"I find . . . offensive, and I would like you to stop immediately."
"If [it doesn't stop/I don't receive redress], I'll file a complaint with. . . ."

Edith: Yes?

You: About that sales manager's position in the eastern region—I think I should've gotten it.

Edith: Well, you know we're trying to bring new blood, new ideas, and new energy into the sales division. Tommy brings all three.

You: I bring experience, contacts, influence, a successful sales record, and previous management experience. I think they should count for something.

Edith: We made our choice on the basis of meeting the standards we set.

You: Which were . . . ?

Edith [*impatiently*]: I told you: new blood, new ideas, and new energy.

You: Code words for "youth," I'm afraid.

Edith: I didn't say that!

You: I told you before, after a pep talk you gave two weeks ago, that you're carrying a smoking gun. Several times you talked about replacing older people with younger ones. On a number of occasions since I've known you, you've referred to me as old, and each time I've asked you to stop. Now you've promoted someone with a fraction of my qualifications into a management position without seriously considering my application.

Edith: I looked at your credentials.

You: I didn't get an interview with anyone: not you, not with the regional vice president. How seriously did you consider my application?

Edith: You're not qualified.

You: Edith, let me spell out my position. I believe I'm experiencing discrimination on the basis of age. I've told you I'm offended by the way you talk to me and talk down to me. I'm offended by the treatment I received during the selection of the regional sales manager, and I resent being passed over without due consideration.

Edith [*sarcastically*]: Planning to sue?

You: The thought has entered my mind.

Edith: Are you threatening me?

You: I've already written my statement for the president of the company, including formal documentation of my charges, with a copy to the vice president of human resources. If I don't get a redress of grievance here, they'll receive it in the company's afternoon mail. I might just take you and the company to court if nothing comes out of any of this.

Edith [*losing her temper*]: Get out of here, old man.

You [*pointing to Edith's secretary sitting just outside the open door*]: This isn't the first time someone has heard you call me that.

Confronting a Man Sexually Harassing A Woman—Stopping a Hostile Environment

You personally don't have to be the object of discrimination or harassment in order to take steps to stop it. In fact, you may be obligated by law to try to stop it when you know it's happening, even if you're not a manager. In this sort of situation:

1. Confront the offending person with your opinions and your feelings.
2. Spell out the circumstances of the person's offensive behavior and the consequences if that behavior doesn't stop.
3. Document your discussion.

Scenario—Stopping a Hostile Environment

Phil has strong opinions about women in the field service crew: "It's a man's job fixing those machines out there." He also has a one-track mind about women: "They're bedmates, not repairmen." And he doesn't cut anyone any slack. You, a man, transferred into the unit recently.

Key Phrases
Confronting Someone about Harassing Others

"I personally don't like the way you talk about. . . ."
"I'm personally offended by the jokes you tell."
"I don't like the way you treat. . . ."
"The behavior I've witnessed is unacceptable to me."
"I wish you'd stop. . . ."
"You can get in trouble, and if I don't say anything, I can get in trouble, too."
"What you're doing is in violation of company policy."
"If you don't stop, I'll. . . ."

Phil: Well, you've been here, what? Six weeks?

You: Yes, just about that.

Phil: What do you think of the guys? Great bunch, aren't they?

You: Yes, they are. Every one of the people in this unit knows his or her job, and does it well. The other night, in the rain, when that rig out there caught fire—I never saw anything like the way everyone pulled together.

Phil: Yeah, a great bunch of guys. I wish to hell they'd get the women out of here, though.

You: I've noticed you're not too happy having women in the unit.

Phil: Big breasts and big machines don't mix. Like alcohol and driving.

You: I don't see it that way. I want to talk to you about it, and I hope we can agree that you should back off the women. In fact, I'm personally offended by your jokes about women and your man-handling the women in the crew. I'm also concerned that what looks like harassment to me can get us *all* in trouble, unless one of us does something about it.

Phil: You going to do something about it? Those broads are too scared of us to say anything.

You: I heard two of the women just this morning shouting at you about what you said to them. I don't think they liked the names you call them—and neither do I. That's why I'm doing something about it right now by talking to you.

Phil: Just what's wrong with calling a girl "honey" or "sweetie"? I call my wife "Babe," and she doesn't complain. She likes it. She'd be mad at me if I didn't.

You: She's your wife. She have a pet name for you?

Phil [*laughing*]: Yeah. But it's none of your business.

You: None of those women are your wife. Besides, you call them a lot more unacceptable names than "honey" and "sweetie." Your words offend me too.

Phil: Hey, what's with you? You one of those feminists?

You: I'm just a guy who thinks your language is out of place. I think that grabbing a woman's backside, for which you're slapped in the face, is out of place and uncalled for.

Phil: You got a bitch, write a letter to the editor, you bleedin' heart.

You: Phil, the women have complained to the crew chief, who thinks you're a card and won't do anything. Maybe if I talk to him, he'll change his mind about things. I don't think he understands the trouble you're going to get him into. If he doesn't do anything, we'll just have to take the problem upstairs.

Phil: Listen, troublemaker. Keep your nose out of this, or I'll take care of you too!

You: Phil, you don't intimidate me the way you do the women. You probably can beat my butt, but I've gotta tell you, I won't sit by while this is going on. And, if you do beat my butt, you'd better make sure I can't ever walk and talk again because I'll take you up on assault charges.

Phil: You're a great talker, but I'd better not hear about you talking with anybody about this.

You: Think about what I've said, Phil. You keep this up, and I think you'll pay dearly for it, and so will the company.

Phil: Sez you!

Conclusion

Not every story has a happy ending, and when you're dealing with conflicts of values and beliefs, you often have to settle for what you can get. By the way, the last two dialogs didn't end with those conversations. They are based on actual court cases in which the plaintiffs won in trial court and on appeal. (These and other similar situations are covered in my book *Fair, Square, and Legal* [AMA-COM, 1990].) In the next chapter, we'll take a more positive look at resolving conflicts and building relationships.

Chapter 12

Investigating
Harassment Claims

Talk to three people who were in the same room in which an incident of some kind occurred, and you're likely to hear about three different events. Multiply the number of people, and you'll probably multiply the number of different stories. Yet, as a manager, you're responsible for getting to the bottom of a complaint of harassment.

Sexual harassment is a high-visibility issue today, and the dialogs in this chapter chronicle interviews with people involved in one such incident. That doesn't mean that other forms of harassment don't exist or are less important. On the contrary, the emergence of sexual harassment from the office supply closet has focused attention on a whole range of business terrorism: racial, ethnic, religious, age, physical, and emotional/mental disabilities. These abuses of people who are different, weaker, or more easily intimidated have always happened. Now, they're no longer allowed.

Equal employment opportunity laws and sexual harassment guidelines instruct managers on how to conduct themselves during an investigation. I recommend you read Ellen J. Wagner's book on the subject, *Sexual Harassment in the Workplace: How to Prevent, Investigate, and Resolve Problems in Your Organization* (AMACOM, 1992), as well as my own book, *Fair, Square, and Legal* (AMACOM, 1990).

Investigating a Charge of Sexual Harassment—Angry Woman

Harassment. There's a legal definition for it (the underlying assumption of these dialogs): any form of unsolicited, unwelcome, offensive behavior (including verbal behavior) that makes a reasonable person's working conditions difficult to the point of interfering with the person's ability to do the job effectively. Such behavior must have been protested in some manner.

In its subtlest forms, harassment arises when a value system holds that one person is inferior to another. These subtle forms of harassment—condescension, verbal abuse, exclusion, tokenism—are found in every form of *-ism*. When it comes to harassment as creating a hostile environment, a single incident or isolated incidents of offensive conduct or remarks generally do not create a hostile environment unless the conduct is severe. In *most* cases, the courts will rule that a hostile environment exists only when there is a pattern of unreasonable conduct. On the other hand, a single incident of quid pro quo harassment is sufficient to warrant charges. *Quid pro quo* refers to making submitting to sexual demands an implicit or explicit term or condition of employment or of management decisions with regard to salaries or promotions.

When investigating a claim of harassment, keep these rules in mind:

- Harassment is in the eye of the beholder. Take care to uncover the alleged harasser's true intentions: friendliness, thoughtlessness, innocent remarks, bids for attention—or genuine abuse.
- Ask the person making the complaint to be specific and objective.
- Don't put words in the mouth of the person alleging harassment by asking laundry-list or multiple-choice questions.
- Get all the facts needed for an investigation: the frequency of the harassment, the length of time it has been going on, the steps the person complaining has taken to let the other person know that she is offended and wants the behavior to stop.
- Ask for witnesses' names or for corroborating evidence.
- Find out what the person expects or wants you to do next (and do not ask leading questions, such as, "Do you want a transfer?").
- Ask for permission to conduct a thorough investigation. If the person denies permission because of fears of reprisal,

give reassurance that no reprisals will occur for bringing the complaint or for permitting an investigation.
- Contact the right officer in your organization for instructions on how to proceed and how to apply the organization's harassment policies properly.

The three-part dialog that follows creates a composite dramatization of several real situations. First, you'll see how to handle the complaint; then how to question the alleged harasser; and, finally, how to question a possible witness. All three components are essential to a thorough investigation.

Scenario—Angry Woman

Stella had complained in the past that several men on her shift not only didn't take her seriously but flagrantly and unreasonably interfered with her ability to do her job, you found out after being hired from outside the company to manage a large distribution center. They intimidated her daily with offensive jokes; left "girlie" magazines open on the table in the break room and compared her figure with the models'; drew lewd caricatures of her on wall posters; propositioned her. "All in fun," the men protested—and no one in management followed up on the charges.

Now Stella is hopping mad. Two hours prior to the start of her shift, she showed up in your office with another complaint. The shift supervisor told her last night that if she wanted to keep her job, she'd have to have sex with him.

You know that if this is true, this constitutes a case of quid pro quo. The company has already left itself wide open to a major lawsuit by failing to stop the harassment; if it does nothing now, it will put a nail in its own coffin. The hostile environment charge is bad enough, but this new complaint spells big trouble. How do you determine the truth of the charges?

Key Phrases
Probing the Charges

"Tell me your side of the story."
"What did you do when. . . ?"

"How often has this happened?"
"When did it first happen?"
"Who else was [involved/present]?"
"How do you feel about my investigating this?"

Stella: I've had it! If something isn't done now, I'm going straight from here to a lawyer. Today!

You: You seem quite angry! [*Pointing to the small conference table and closing the door against the warehouse noise:*] Come in, and let's talk about it. [*You both sit at the table.*]

Stella: Angry? You bet I'm angry! I'm living a nightmare here.

You: Tell me more.

Stella [*calming down a little*]: I spent the night figuring out what to do. The couple of nights you spent down here, everyone was on their best behavior. Last night [*tears coming to her eyes*] it reached the lowest point ever. It's gotten so bad, I can't talk about it without bawling.

You: Please, Stella. I want to hear about it.

Stella: The guys make my life living hell. I'm the first woman in this warehouse, and they don't like it—and I'm not just guessing at that. They've told me straight out. But more important, they call me "tramp" and "whore" because I work nights and with men. They say they're only making jokes, but I don't find them funny. They leave pictures of naked women on the tables. They draw nasty pictures with my name on it.

You: How long has this been going on?

Stella: I've been here eight months. It's been going on eight months.

You: What have you done about it personally?

Stella: I've told them to stop. I've *begged* them to stop. I talked with the manager before you lots of times. All he ever said was, "Boys'll be boys. Ignore them and they'll stop." He offered to switch me to days if an opening ever came up, but none ever did.

You: So when these things happen, you tell the guys that you're offended, that you want all this to stop, but protesting only seems to egg them on. Do I understand you correctly?

Stella: You got it. [*After a slight pause:*] But do you really care?

You: I do. I don't like what I'm hearing, and I want to get to the bottom of it. But you said something happened last night that really upsets you more than anything else.

Stella [*tears coming back to her eyes*]: Yeah. Oh, man. How do I say it? You probably won't believe me. Jason, the shift supervisor. He did things to me. He said things to me.

You [*after a brief silence*]: Tell me what happened, even though it's hard for you. As hard as it may be, please be as specific as you can be.

Stella [*angrily*]: You want all the details?

You: I need to hear what I have to deal with. Tell me what you can, the best you can. Take your time, and tell it in your own way.

Stella [*calmer*]: Last night, I came on at five o'clock, like I always do. A bunch of the guys were standing around laughing and joking, like they usually do. They were watching me come in and laughing a lot. One of them called out, "Get any good loving today?" Well, that wasn't his exact word. I just walked on by. Another guy said, "Well, if you ain't getting any good loving, you're going to get some now."

They go on like that all the time, so I didn't pay any attention. Did my job. When my first break came, I went into the break room. The same bunch of guys were there—and Jason. Well, those guys left when I came in, and Jason stayed behind.

You [*after Stella stopped talking and looked down at her hands*]: What happened then?

Stella [*making cold eye contact*]: You're not going to believe me, and if you do, you'll probably pass it off as just a guy thing.

You: Stella, let me assure you that I want to know what happened so I can do what I can to help you. What would you like me to do?

Stella: Make them stop. For what he did last night, you should fire him, but I'd be happy if you just make Jason leave me alone.

You: Unless you tell me your version of what happened, I won't be able to do any of that. If what you tell me is true, I intend to take action immediately.

Stella [*alarmed*]:   What do you mean *if* it's true? Of course, it's true. Do you think I'd make up something like this?

You: I understand you're angry, but until I investigate your claims, I have no way of taking the appropriate action. I want to help you, but I have to make sure that what I'm doing will give you the right kind of help. I'm here to listen to you, Stella—with an open mind.

Stella [*with tears in her eyes*]:   Look, I'm no kid virgin, but nobody's ever done this to me before, and nothing like this has ever happened. [*After a brief silence:*] He made a few comments about me looking good. I had my hair fixed yesterday. I thanked him, and then he said things like I'm looking good enough to eat for dinner and stuff like that. I told him to stop, and if he didn't stop I'd take my break elsewhere. But he got up from the table and turned off the lights. It was pitch black in there—no windows, the door closed. Since you put the candy and drink machines outside the door to make room for some extra tables, there's no light in there at all.

   I don't know how he found me in the dark, but suddenly he was there, and his hands were on my shoulders. He pulled me back against him and slipped his hand into my shirt and under my bra. He told me how much he really likes me and how much he wanted to have sex with me and how we could do it right then.

   [*crying openly*] I pulled out of his hands and banged myself on the table. It still hurts where I hit myself. He tried to sweet-talk me into doing it, but I told him no. I told him *never*. I called him some real foul names to make it clear I think he's a creep and a bastard. But I couldn't find my way out of the room. I went the wrong way, bumped into some chairs and the wall. I couldn't find the door. That's when he told me I'd better give in to him because, if I didn't, he'd have my job.

You [*after Stella quit talking and cried softly for a minute*]:   What did you tell him then?

Stella: "Let me outta here and I'll think about it." I had to do something. I had to say something quick. I was scared silly. Jason's a big man. I'm strong, but I can't take on a man that big and beat him. But that's what the guys meant when they said I'd be getting some good—loving—from now on. *He told them what he was going to do!*

You: Let me ask you again, Stella. What action do you want me to take?

Stella: Fire Jason and make the other guys leave me alone. That's what I want to see happen.

You: What do you want me to do as a next step?

Stella: Go ahead, talk to Jason. He'll deny it, but it's all true.

You: A thorough investigation will take a few days and may be painful. How do you feel about my making some inquiries?

Stella: If you do, you'd be the first.

You: You're willing, then?

Stella: Ready and able!

You: Please be sure of this because I'm going to have to ask you some hard questions that could make you very angry with me, but I have to ask them.

Stella: You seem on the level. So, ask me your questions. Then ask the same kind of questions of Jason. You'll see who's telling the truth.

You: Stella, have you ever given Jason any reason to believe that you are willing to have sex with him?

Stella [*reddening*]: No.

You: Have you ever bantered, told sexually-oriented jokes, or laughed at those jokes with the guys?

Stella: No. I don't like those kinds of jokes. They're always saying nasty things about women. They don't belong in this warehouse. They want to tell filthy jokes, take them to the barroom.

You: Just for the record, what do you tell them?

Stella: I tell them to stop. I tell them their jokes aren't funny. I tell them that their jokes disgust me. You should see some of the pictures they leave around.

You: Do you have any?

Stella: Would you believe me if I showed them to you? That they left them on the table?

You: Why would I doubt your word?

Stella: The last manager did. [*After a slight pause:*] But I got some. They're in a file I'm going to give to a lawyer if you don't do anything.

You: Just who were the other men you were talking about?

Stella: I'm going to get in trouble for this, aren't I?

You: What do you mean?

Stella: You're going to tell those guys what I said, and they're going to give me a bad time.

You: Not if I can help it, Stella. No one will hurt you because you made this complaint. This inquiry will be fair and impartial. If anyone gets on to you about it, let me know immediately, and I'll put a stop to it. I need to talk with them. How do you feel about what I've said?

Stella: You're a whole hell of a lot better than the last person I complained to. [*After a slight pause:*] Allen, Charlie, Bill, and Frank— they're the other guys.

You: Stella, these are the steps I'm going to take. I'm going to talk with the men, starting with Jason. Please don't discuss this with them. If you can, go about your work as normal.

Stella: If I have to.

You: I think it would be best if you can, but the decision is yours.

Stella: Okay. As long as you do something quick.

You: I'll talk with Jason as soon as he comes in. We always meet before the shift begins.

Investigating a Charge of Sexual Harassment—Defensive Alleged Harasser

To prevent being held liable for the acts of other people, you need to investigate claims of harassment thoroughly. Although the U.S. Supreme Court hedged on employer liability when it said employers are not automatically liable for the actions of their supervisors, both you and your company must take any complaint seriously and at face value until its satisfactory conclusion. The courts expect managers to carry out a thorough investigation of any claim, and they expect prompt remedial action. If it's true that the complaining employee had been coerced, propositioned, placed in a threatening situation, or experienced a job detriment, promising to transfer the offended party or slapping the offender's wrist may not be sufficient; the punishment should fit the crime.

A manager's response to a hostile environment in which sexual, racial, or any other form of harassment exists must be swift and sure in order to maintain a productive, profitable work environment—one in which all personnel feel safe from harm and from unreasonable interference with work performance. Thus, in these situations:

- Take a complaint of harassment seriously and act professionally, even if a story of sexual harassment appears sensational or titillating.
- Give the victim a fair hearing. Give the alleged harasser the same fairness.

Even if, in a case of sexual harassment, the complaining person seems to have consented, sexual behavior often results from fear rather than agreement, and a complaining employee may have held back a complaint for fear of retaliation.

Scenario—Defensive Alleged Harasser

Jason comes to work at 4:30 P.M. to meet with you for at least a half-hour before the evening shift begins. Today he comes in a few minutes earlier and seems totally unaware of any problem. After a few minutes of small talk, you begin your inquiry.

Key Phrases
Talking to the Alleged Harasser

"I need to talk with you about something I heard."
"What happened [with reference to a time or place the alleged event took place]?"
"What's your side of the story?"

"I need to pursue this charge to the end in order to make a fair
   determination of the facts and a fair disposition of the case."
"I'll be talking with other people about this. Is there someone
   you think I should talk to?"

You: Jason, instead of our regular meeting agenda, I have to talk
   with you about something.

Jason: Oh?

You: I'm not going to beat around the bush. A charge of sexual
   harassment has been brought against you, and I want to—

Jason [*interrupting*]:   That Stella again! She's always trying to get me
   into trouble. Hey! I'm a married man. I get plenty of good sex at
   home. Why'd I want to mess around with that woman?

You: No one said you did. [*slight pause*] Jason, this conversation is
   between you and me, unless for some reason it has to go beyond
   this level. I have to chase down everything because the charges
   are serious, and I want to make sure that everyone—you and
   Stella and anyone else—is treated fairly. Maybe *you* should tell
   me what happened last night.

Jason [*belligerently*]:   Nothing.

You: Stella says differently.

Jason: What does she say?

You: Before I tell you that, Jason, I'd like to hear your side of the
   story.

Jason: There's nothing to hear. After you left, I came out on the
   floor. Everyone was here working. We did our jobs and we went
   home.

You: How about during the first break?

Jason: The first break. [*After a pregnant silence:*] I don't know what
   she told you happened, but I wasn't going to say anything because I didn't want to get her in trouble. So much for being Mis-
   ter Nice Guy.

You: You're suggesting that she said or did something.

Jason: Yeah. She came on to me big time. Last night we were alone
   in the break room, and she says to me, "Look, Jason. The guys'll

leave me alone if they think we got something going. They wouldn't mess with you. So why don't we do it?" She wanted me to have sex with her right there in the break room.

You: What did you say?

Jason: I said, "Hey! You're just asking for trouble. You can't make suggestions to me like that. Number one, I'm a happily married man. And, number two, I'd get my ass in a sling if I did any of those things to a subordinate."

You: So, you're saying that she propositioned you?

Jason: Yeah.

You: Who else knows about this?

Jason: What kind a guy you take me for? I didn't tell anyone. Jeeze!

You: So it's her word against yours.

Jason: That's the way it is.

You: Is there anything else you want to say about that specific charge?

Jason: Hell no! There's nothing more to say. Like I told you. She came on to me with this cockamamy story of hers.

You: What about her complaint that the men were bothering her? What did you say to that?

Jason: She blows everything out of proportion! All those feminists do.

You: So let's talk about those things. What is she complaining about?

Jason: That the guys tell her dirty jokes, that they give her pictures of naked girls, especially crotch shots. Allen, he's a great cartoonist, and he drew a picture of her she called dirty and pulled it off the wall and tore it up.

You: So all those stories are true.

Jason: Yeah, but she blows them out of proportion. It's all in fun. No one's trying to hurt her.

You: What do you tell the guys?

Jason: What do you mean?

You: What do you tell them about their behavior?

Jason: I've told them to ease off, but you know guys. They're just having fun.

You: Then, if I understand you, Stella's complaint that those things go on is true, and you haven't put a stop to it.

Jason: That's not the way it really is. But I guess that's what you want me to do: put a stop to her complaints.

You: I want the men to stop telling dirty jokes in the warehouse or anywhere else that Stella or I are present. I want you to tell them to stop doing it. I want you to prevent them from bothering her again. It's company policy and it's human decency to treat that woman with the same dignity and respect you expect for yourself.

Jason [*angrily*]: So you're taking her word against mine?

You: No. I'm taking your word for the harassment you said goes on out there. As for the charges against you personally, the jury's still out on that one. Put a stop to the harassment, Jason. In the meantime, I've told the dispatcher to ask each of the men to come and talk with me privately.

Jason: You think I harassed her last night. What did she tell you?

You: She said you trapped her in the break room after the men left. Turned off the lights, grabbed her, fondled her, and threatened her job if she didn't have sex with you every night.

Jason [*exploding*]: Damn! *What lies!* That's what she'd like me to do, but I wouldn't do anything like that.

You: That's what I want to find out, Jason. I want to know the truth as much as you want me to know it. These are very serious charges. Is there anyone in particular you want me to talk to?

Jason: No one was in the room with us.

You: Anyone to corroborate your story?

Jason: No one, I guess. Whatever you've been writing down, I guess that's all I got on my side.

You: While I'm looking into this, I have to ask you to please leave the premises right now. Take the night off, with pay. I'll call you at home in the morning.

Investigating a Charge of Sexual Harassment—Reluctant Witness

Talking with witnesses can be as difficult as talking with the principals in the case. Following these guidelines will help you get the information you need:

- Talk in private, promise as much confidentiality as is possible under the circumstances, and promise that no reprisals will take place.
- Don't confront or be combative, especially in public.
- Don't make light of the situation or minimize its importance or seriousness.
- Come directly to the point—for example, "You were identified as a witness to an incident last night, and I'd like us to discuss the matter."
- Maintain objectivity; be as unbiased as possible; don't take sides, talk about rumors as if they are facts, or preach.
- Inquire into the history and circumstances of the complaint, asking about what the witness might have seen or heard.
- Don't ask the witness to make assumptions, offer opinions, or pass judgment about the situation or the people involved.
- Keep the discussion on track. Don't get sidetracked.

Scenario—Reluctant Witness

Charlie is the first to arrive at work and come into the office. He senses something is wrong because being summoned to the manager's office is not a common occurrence. When it does happen, it's because a problem does exist.

Key Phrases
Talking to a Witness

"You've been identified as a witness to something that happened."

"I need to talk to you about anything you might have seen or heard."

"Unless anything comes of these charges and you're asked to talk with other people, everything you say will be in strict confidence."

"What did you see or hear?"

"No one will take reprisal against you for anything you have to say."

Charlie [*from the doorway; nervous*]:   You wanted to see me?

You: Yes. Come in, Charlie. [*Motioning to the chair at the conference table where you are already seated:*] Have a seat. How are you tonight?

Charlie: I'm fine.

You: You seem tense, but this isn't really about you. You've been identified as a witness in a situation, and I want to talk to you about anything you might know about it. Anything you say will be held in confidence unless we have to take the situation to a higher level. And then we'll ask you to cooperate if it's necessary. Okay?

Charlie: I didn't see or hear anything last night.

You: Last night?

Charlie: You were talking about last night, weren't you?

You: Did something happen last night I should know about?

Charlie: Naw. Just another night in the warehouse.

You: That's not what I've been told. Stella has charged Jason with a serious sexual offense. She thinks you know something about it. Jason denies the charge. What you have to say could help me decide on the truth.

Charlie: Nothing happened. [*After a pregnant pause:*] I didn't see or hear anything. [*After a slight pause:*] Do I need a lawyer?

You: I'm not charging you with anything, Charlie. I just want to get at the truth. You're just a possible witness. Just describe what happened here last night.

Charlie: I got to work at a few minutes before five. Had a soft drink with Allen and Frank and went to work. That's it. Jason stopped to talk a few minutes, but then he had to come in here.

You: What happened when Stella came to work?

Charlie: Nothing.

You: What did you say to her?

Charlie: Hi.

You: That's it?

Charlie: Yeah. We don't talk to her very much. She doesn't like us.

You: How come?

Charlie: Beats me. [*After a pregnant silence:*] She doesn't like our sense of humor. I think it's a chronic case of PMS.

You: Your sense of humor. What's that like, Charlie?

Charlie: You know. Guy talk. Jokes, sex, ball games. Stuff like that.

You: You tell jokes she doesn't like?

Charlie: Yeah. Sometimes. She's just a prude.

You: She's asked you to stop telling jokes?

Charlie: Yeah.

You: Have you stopped?

Charlie: No. Why should we? It's just one of her and four of us. If she doesn't like our jokes, she doesn't have to listen to them!

You: Let's talk about what happened during the first break last night.

Charlie: Nothing. Me and Allen and Frank and Jason were in the break room a few minutes. It was hot in there. We decided to leave. Just then Stella came in. I didn't see or hear nothing in that room.

You: What was there to see or hear?

Charlie: Nothing.

You: What did either Stella or Jason tell you about what happened in that room?

Charlie [*visibly upset*]: That they talked.

You: What did he say they talked about?

Charlie [*fighting for composure*]: Things. [*after a pregnant silence:*] Things. [*another pause:*] Do I have to tell you what he told me?

You: Better to tell me than to have to tell someone else.

Charlie [*struggling*]: He—he said . . . Oh damn, I can't tell you what he said. Besides, he was probably just bragging.

You: If he was, no one has anything to worry about.

Charlie: He said he would be getting sex from her every night.

You: That's what he told you.

Charlie: Yeah. But I didn't believe him.

You: Why would he tell you that if it weren't true?

Charlie: Because he told us when we first came on that tonight's the night he gets sex from her.

You: That's what he told you.

Charlie: Yeah, but you know guys. More talk than action.

You: Thanks, Charlie. As I said, this doesn't affect you directly. But I'd like you to take the night off, with pay. Leave the warehouse now, and don't talk to anyone on your way out.

Charlie: Who'll do the work tonight?

You: Don't worry about it. We'll handle things here.

Conclusion

In a similar court case, "Stella" brought charges against the company. The real "Jason" admitted that "Stella's" story was true, and the company had to pay "Stella" heavy damages. All of this could have been prevented with written, enforceable, and enforced policies prohibiting harassment of any kind. Companies need to give all managers training on how to enforce those policies, how to conduct investigations, and what to do if harassment is charged.

Chapter 13
Building Relationships

What do you say when you want to build a business-related, personal relationship with someone you work with? Try it with one employee, and the other employees may think you play favorites; the person you want the relationship with may be suspicious of your motives. Peers may be competitive and want to hold you at arm's length. Your boss might think you're buttering up to him. A vendor may think you're trying to take advantage of her. And anyone might think you're "coming on" sexually. These are all common fears. Yet open, friendly relationships make the workplace a better place and will even boost productivity. So what do you do?

I have one general rule to follow with employees: Be friendly with everyone. I also have a general rule to follow with peers: Be friendly with everyone. And my general rule to follow with my boss when I worked in a corporate environment was: Be friendly with everyone. Although I don't treat everyone alike, I let everyone know that I'm open and available to anyone.

Now that doesn't mean that I like everyone; I'm no Will Rogers (who said he never met a man he didn't like). Rather, in a working environment, I try to create a climate in which everyone feels accepted and valued for what she can do and the contribution she can make.

Building a Relationship with an Employee Suspicious of Your Motives

Creating a friendly, open environment begins with you. People will respond in kind, whether they realize it or not. Here are some ways to warm the atmosphere of your workplace:

- Smile appropriately; be genuine and sincere (phoniness or manipulation can be spotted a mile off).
- Use names when talking with others.
- Offer to help others, and follow through on the offer.
- Accept help from others; solicit it when you need it.
- Use *please* and *thank you*.
- Greet people warmly.
- Keep your personal problems to yourself, unless asked to talk about them.
- Listen to other people's problems.
- Compliment people when they do something well.
- Recognize people as people, and treat them with dignity.

Scenario—Employee Suspicious of Your Motives

You quickly realized, after taking over the department as its supervisor, that Monica, a young African-American woman, could easily run the show. Although she hadn't applied for the position when it was vacant, she is brimming with good ideas, quick to solve problems, fun to be around, and liked by everyone. You want to build a relationship with her, but Monica seems reluctant. After weeks of trying to be friendly, an opportunity arose to talk about what was happening.

Key Phrases
Building a Relationship with an Employee

"Please . . . thank you."
"I'd like to hear your opinions about. . . ."
"How can I help you do. . . ?"
"Here's something that I think you might enjoy doing; and it'll be a big help to me."
"It'll help me if I know more about you."
"Thanks for telling me more about yourself. I'd like you to know a few things about me, too."

You: I'm glad this project's over and done with. I appreciate the work you did, Monica. It saved us a lot of time, and it was very creative. And working with you was fun.

Monica: I'm glad it's done. I guess I had fun too.

You [*after an uncomfortable pause*]: It seems to me that you're troubled by something.

Monica: No, I'm not.

You: Maybe it seems that way to me because *I'm* troubled by something. It seems you're holding me at arm's length and not letting me get close. Mind if we talk about it, Monica?

Monica [*surprised, suspicious*]: You're my boss. What more is there?

You: Okay. As a boss, how do you see me?

Monica: I guess you're all right, as far as bosses go. I've had worse.

You [*lightly*]: Well, I'm glad I'm not the *worst*. Monica, sometimes a little feedback helps the boss do the job better, too. I've been here for a few months, and I don't know how I'm doing as far as everyone's concerned. I'm bothered too by the fact that being friendly with you hasn't been too successful.

Monica: *You* want feedback from *me.*

You: Sure.

Monica: And you want to be *friends* with me.

You: *Friends* might be a strong word, but I would like to see a friendlier relationship. Does it bother you to give me a little feedback about how you see me doing as the supervisor?

Monica: No, I guess it won't hurt, because I think you're doing a pretty good job. If I didn't think that, I probably wouldn't tell you anything. But don't let that go to your head!

You [*laughing*]: I'll try to stay humble, Monica. Anything specific you want to tell me?

Monica: You seem to like us and respect us, and that counts a lot. You know your job, and you do it well. I suppose the thing I like best is that you let us do our jobs, and you ask us to do more than our last supervisor did.

You: Too much?

Monica: Oh, no. It's pretty good stuff, like this project we just did.

You: That it?

Monica: I guess so.

You: I'm glad to hear that I'm okay, as far as bosses go, but I'm still puzzled as to why I feel you're distant. You banter and laugh a lot with the other people, but when I'm around, you quiet down. You don't joke and kid around with me the way you do with the others.

Monica [*insistently*]: You're the boss.

You: So, my being the boss is a barrier to you. It's not something I've done or said?

Monica: Not at all. But the boss is the boss, and that's the way it's gotta be.

You: What if I told you that I don't like bosses who want to be treated that way—that they're the boss and that's the way it's gotta be?

Monica: You don't?

You: I know what you're talking about, Monica. I've had bosses like that. My boss now doesn't treat me that way, and I wouldn't have taken this job if I felt he would be like that.

Monica: I wish I knew what you're talking about.

You: Before I became a boss I was a person. In fact, I'm *still* a person, just as you are, and that's the way I'd like to be seen. We don't have to be friends, Monica, but I'd sure like us to be friendly. Joke around, tell stories about ourselves, just be people working together. I'd like that kind of rapport with everyone, and I think I've got it with most people but not with you. I'm going to ask you straight out, and I hope you don't take it the wrong way. Has it anything to do with race or gender or any other thing different about us?

Monica [*softly*]: Maybe a little, but it's truly only because you're the boss, and I'm not comfortable with you. I'm not used to supervisors like you, and, to tell the truth, I haven't trusted you. It seems as if you're trying to get too close to everyone just so you can get more work out of them.

You: That I'm manipulating people?

Monica: That's what I've been thinking, but I could be wrong. I'll need a little time to think about this conversation. I don't trust people easily—not just you, but most people, and I especially don't trust supervisors all that much.

You: I'll try to earn your trust, Monica. I don't expect that merely talking about it will change anything, but I want you to know I'm sincere in what I've said today, and I hope you'll take it in the manner in which I intended.

Building a Relationship with a Competitive Peer

The organizational climate in some workplaces often pits peers against one another, making it very difficult to develop good relationships. Even if your workplace fosters good interpersonal relations, some people have been "coached" by other environments to distrust and compete with their peers. The next promotion may be at stake; the "leg up" may be pulled out from under you. Any number of competitive attitudes may flourish unless you take steps to prevent the competition from alienating you from your coworkers. Especially in an environment that encourages teamwork, making "friends" with peers becomes essential. You can foster these relationships:

- Give people time to get to know and trust you before you become too assertive.
- Be open and receptive to feedback from others.
- Give feedback constructively and helpfully.
- Be supportive.
- Ask for support in matters that don't threaten other people.
- Be helpful and ask for help.
- Share information and opinions; ask for information and opinions when appropriate.

Scenario—Competitive Peer

Jack came into the unit three weeks after you did. Both of you are specialists, and both of you manage a small team of people doing closely related work. You manage the A Team and Jack the B Team. Your manager, a vice president, is due to retire within the next two or three years. Both of you are in line for that position, and both of you want it. Jack seems to want it in the "worst way" because he has been playing politics with members of the executive committee, withholding information you need, and in other ways interfering with your ability to work with him. The conflict has been showing up in cross-functional team meetings and in staff meetings with your manager. After a particularly stressful staff meeting, when it became clear for the first time that Jack has been withholding critical information that your team needs, you feel compelled to discuss the situation with him.

Key Phrases
Dealing with a Competitive Peer

"I know we're looking to get the same . . . and I think we need to talk about it."
"I'm becoming angry that. . . ."
"I'd like us to talk about how things are going between us."
"How do you see the situation here?"
"What suggestions do you have to. . . ?"
"What would like to see happen?"

You: I think we need to talk, Jack.

Jack: What about?

You: How do you feel about the relationship you and I have?

Jack: You manage the A Team, I manage the B Team, and between the two we get the job done.

You: A Team's not been getting the job done lately, and this afternoon, during the staff meeting, you talked about some things that we needed to know before this. Without that information, we stalled out.

Jack: Well, now you've got it. So what's the problem?

You: That information should've been on my desk over a week ago, Jack. I couldn't help but notice that the report you received from the vendor and that you passed around today was dated more two weeks ago. Please explain that to me.

Jack: I don't have to answer to you.

You: I'm going to be straight and up-front with you, Jack, because that's the way I'd like us to be. I know we're competing to get the boss's job when he retires, but I think you're going about it the wrong way.

Jack: I don't have to listen to this.

You: Please hear me out. It's important to me, but I think it's also important to the company, and it's most important to the members of the A Team. Anything you do to hurt me will hurt those people more than it'll hurt me. I want the VP position, but I won't go for it at the expense of my people or *yours.* And I'd appreciate it very much if we resolve this now—and once and for all!

Jack: You're really ticked off, aren't you?

You: Yes, I am.

Jack [*after a pregnant silence*]: So, what do you want from me?

You: What do you think we can do to get past this and work together again, the way we should?

Jack: I want that job.

You: I know you do, and so do I.

Jack: Only one of us can get it.

You: I know that, too.

Jack [*laughing*]: So I'll just have to bump you off! [*You remain silent.*] You didn't think that was funny. I guess it wasn't. [*After a pregnant silence:*] You want me to ease up. Play fair. That it?

You: That's it in a nutshell because if I don't think you are playing fair, we'll have to decide who'll tell the boss that you're withholding information the A Team needs to do its job—or whatever else it is that you're doing to put hurdles in my way. I don't think he'd like it if he found out that our productivity is being sabotaged. It's his bottom line, you know. I think it'll serve your interest more to play fair than to play dirty. The consequences of playing cut-throat could be severe.

Jack: Man, you're cold.

You: So, what do you think?

Jack: It's in my court, isn't it?

You: That's the way I see it.

Jack: What do *you* want me to do? [*After a pregnant silence:*] I guess I shouldn't have asked that. Okay. I'll back off, but I'll do anything fair and square to get that job.

You: That's all right with me because that's what I'm going to do, too. I don't expect you to help me get the promotion, Jack, but I don't want to see you interfering with my team again. This is a business, not a football game.

Building a Relationship with Your Boss—A Boss Everyone Else Resents

Making friends with the boss poses its own special problems. How do you do that without looking bad in her eyes as well as in the eyes of other beholders? At the same time, a good relationship helps make the workplace more comfortable for everyone. Here are some hints:

- Be friendly without being pushy.
- Listen to the boss's tales of woe.
- Give the boss credit when credit is due.
- Support the boss in public, but give her honest feedback when it's appropriate.
- Be there when she needs help, but stick to your guns if she overwhelms you with more than you can handle.
- Treat the boss to lunch once in a while, but don't make a show of it.
- Notice little things, and let her know you've noticed—such as her children's accomplishments.

Caveat: You may not want to get close to a boss who manages badly or disregards you as a person. You have to weigh value versus effort.

Scenario—A Boss Everyone Else Resents

You, an underwriting manager, acquired a new boss a few months ago: a pleasant, middle-aged man with outstanding credentials the company hired from the outside, supposedly to prevent unnecessary rivalry among the underwriting managers. You understand that top management thought that no one in the division is qualified to run it. Other managers are still grumbling, and most won't have much to do with the new vice president, but you want to know this person, want to learn from him, and you have told the other managers that ragging him makes *them* look bad. When you speak with them, they seem hardened against the boss, and they've let you know that they won't appreciate it if you "butter up the old boy." Reaffirming their right to their opinions and feelings, you present a contrary position on which you will act. "At least everyone knows where everyone stands."

Key Phrases
Building a Relationship with Your Boss

"At the risk of sounding hokey, what can I do to help?"

"I'd like to know more about you; that way I'll know how to work with you."

"What do you think we can do to become more effective teammates?"

"Sometimes people in your position think it's a bit risky to get too close to employees, but if you ever need to talk to someone about a problem or something, I'd like you to feel that I can keep your confidence."

"I like the way you handled that presentation."

"Thanks for supporting us with the executive committee."

You [*from the boss's open door*]:   Do you have a minute, George?

George: Sure. Come on in. Sit down?

You [*leaving the door open; sitting*]:   Thanks.

George: What can I do for you?

You: Nothing, really. I'd like to do something for you.

George [*puzzled*]:   What's that?

You: You've been here a couple of months, but I don't think anyone's ever welcomed you on board. [*Seeing the boss's face redden:*] I don't mean to embarrass you or upset you . . .

George: No. It's all right. I didn't think anyone noticed, and my impression has been that even though I extended myself to you managers, you weren't open to it.

You: I'll speak only for myself. I should have come in here sooner.

George: That's okay. I understand. But won't people see you as a brown noser or as a stooge or something?

You: They know me better. Being friendly also includes being honest. I'll support you when I can, but if you'll let me, I'll let you know when I don't agree with you. I hope that's okay with you.

George: That's good. That's the way I want it.

You: People here know me as an honest and direct person. The other managers know I'm here to make peace with you, and I hope they'll follow my lead.

Conclusion

Making friends at work can be risky business. On the other hand, a friendly environment rates higher in importance among employees than does the amount of pay. People want to be recognized as people, and they want to be recognized for their achievements. Give recognition to others, and they'll do the same for you.

Section V

Disciplining, Firing, And Implementing A Downsizing Decision

Firing an employee is never easy, especially if you made the hire, because you have to face your own initial decision. Nevertheless, low-performing employees or employees who flaunt the rules hurt your work group's productivity, morale, and relationships with other employees. When performance coaching or behavior counseling fails, it's time to take action. These scripts should help you do it.

Firing someone whose performance doesn't meet standards or whose behavior is unacceptable is hard enough. Laying off people during a downsizing is much more difficult. Then, you have to manage the people who remain behind—the survivors—as well. Downsizing affects everyone, including you. The scripts in this chapter should make it easier to implement the downsizing decision.

Chapter 14

Taking Corrective Action: Performance Probation And Dismissal

Coaching doesn't always help employees improve their performance. Some employees have difficulty catching on to specific areas of a job. Six key conditions may overwhelm any and all coaching efforts, even when coupled with additional training:

1. The employee can't understand the job.
2. The employee doesn't have the knowledge or the skills to do the job well.
3. The employee doesn't want to do the job.
4. The employee has personal problems.
5. The employee is unhappy with the work situation.
6. The employee is unhappy with the quality of supervision.

Some employees don't respond to anything other than threats. They have the knowledge and the skills, but they lack the motivation to change unless you threaten their jobs and security. Their need to be put on the spot requires supervisors to confront them and to impose the need for change rather than merely request it.

Some companies spell out procedures for putting an employee on performance probation, and those policies should be followed to the letter in order to protect you from a serious charge of wrongful management conduct. The three most common steps are oral warning, a written warning with probation, and transfer (if possible) or dismissal. Sometimes, though, there are conditions of performance that could warrant immediate action:

- The employee jeopardizes his own safety or that of other people.
- The employee's work includes very sensitive information that could endanger the organization in some way.
- The employee's lack of skills are too costly to remedy.

If your company has published probationary procedures, ensure that all employees (particularly new employees) know those procedures and under what conditions you will invoke them. A company orientation should explain them; if your organization doesn't have an orientation, you need to take responsibility for spelling out the terms. If you follow your own personal guidelines because your company doesn't have published procedures, let your employees know what to expect. Blindside them, and they'll retaliate in kind.

In all cases, sound business reasons must dictate action. And regardless of the action you decide to take, coordinate with your Human Resources Department (if your company has one) or with the person to whom you report. (If you are a sole proprietor and have any doubts as to the soundness of your reasons or about the legality of your action, consult with your attorney before doing anything.)

Above all, keep your documentation up-to-date. Don't wait until you decide to fire the person to build your file. Keep thorough records about all your employees' performance from the day they come to work for you. Document performance problems and the discussions you've had about them before taking dramatic corrective action. Failure to do so could land you in court, and the court could find against you.

Taking Corrective Action—Oral Warning—The Ideal Situation

If an employee is worth salvaging, it's important to find out why his performance doesn't come up to standard and put him on a reasonable period of performance probation. When you take corrective action:

- Give direct and honest performance feedback in a timely manner so the employee has an opportunity to take corrective action on his own.
- Support the employee's self-esteem by building on positive achievements and strengths, but be firm about the need for change.
- Engage in problem solving with the employee, and coach him appropriately to remedy the situation.
- If initial coaching doesn't help and conditions permit it, give an oral warning, including the consequences of not improving performance and a deadline by when marked improvement should be seen.

Scenario—The Ideal Situation

Bill has been on the job in your marketing department for nearly three months, although he has worked for the company in other capacities for over ten years. The company closed down his part of the business (plant development); instead of building its own units, the company intends to hire outside firms to do the work. Since Bill has been considered a valuable employee, the company decided to give him the option between a severance package or a transfer, and he opted for the latter. Unfortunately, now, in this new position, he may be in over his head.

He is primarily an architectural drafter, not a layout and paste-up artist, which is what you have been asked to have him do. The job is very important, and you need someone in it, but Bill is too slow and doesn't have a clear grasp of the spatial relationships required in the layouts.

Key Phrases
The Oral Warning

"I [we] need. . . ."
"As much as I hate to do this, ..."
"Let me review the standards and other expectations of your job."

"You know the policy, but I'll explain it to make sure we both understand the rules:

- After an oral warning, if your performance doesn't improve, then . . . If it does improve, then. . . .
- A written warning comes after. . . .
- A written warning always includes a statement of probation, and if your performance doesn't improve, then. . . . If it does improve, then. . . .

"Here's what we'll do in the event you have problems learning the job or achieving expectations."

"I don't want to give up on you."

You: Bill, we've talked about this situation on several occasions. I need you to complete these layouts faster. Your layouts are getting better, but I'm still not happy with your artwork. We need other ideas for getting your performance up to standard.

Bill: I'm all out of ideas. I've done everything you and other people have suggested. I've read the texts in the department. I've even done extra reading from the library. Trying to get it right only slows me down more.

You: I'm at a loss, too, and, as much as I hate to do this, Bill, I'm going to have to put you on performance probation until you can get the layouts to me on time. I don't mind tweaking them a bit to get them right, but if they're late, we're all in trouble, including those people downstream in the process. You know the policy here: two weeks from this oral warning to meet our expectations or I have to put you on written notice. Since the job's such a vital one, I'll be able to give you only two weeks more. Then, if a job exists for you, we'll transfer you. If none exists, I'll have to cut you loose. What do you think?

Bill [*dejected*]: What *can* I think? But I understand. I'm probably just at the wrong place at the wrong time.

You: I still don't want to give up on you, Bill, so, here's what I'd like you to do. . . .

Taking Corrective Action—Oral Warning—Angry Employee, Part 1

When an employee accepts an oral warning graciously, the way Bill did, you do little more than design an action plan and execute it. With a belligerent employee, you have to manage the situation much differently:

- Use gatekeepers to let the employee ventilate feelings.
- Use mirroring to let the employee know you understand and acknowledge his feelings.
- Support the employee's self-esteem.
- Maintain your composure at all times, even when expressing anger.
- Be firm in your resolve to take the necessary action, but be fair, caring, and courteous.

Scenario—Angry Employee

The situation is basically the same as in the previous dialog, but the employee isn't cooperative. Having been shifted around during the downsizing, Mike resents the treatment he thinks he's been getting, and he thinks it's only a matter of time before the company will let him go, too. He's told you so very bluntly. Mike has been loyal, more productive than most other employees, and more willing to make the extra effort to get the job done than most other people. Letting him go would be painful to you and to the company, as well as to him.

Key Phrases
Taking Corrective Action with an Angry Employee

"We've talked about this before, and these are the standards that have to be met."
"Here are performance problems on which we have to work."
"I see you're angry about this."
"How do you see the situation?"

"What are the alternatives you see?"
"How can we resolve this together?"
"Here's what I [see/think/feel] about. . . ."

You: Mike, we've talked about this situation on several occasions. I need you to complete these layouts faster. And although the layouts are getting better, I'm still not happy with your artwork. We need other ideas for getting your performance up to standard.

Mike [*short tempered*]:   I'm all out of ideas! I've done everything you and other people have suggested. I've read the texts in the department. I've even done extra reading from the library. Trying to get it right only slows me down more.

You: I'm at a loss, too, and, as much as I hate to do this, Mike, I'm going to have to put you on performance probation until you can get the layouts to me on time. I don't mind tweaking them a bit to get them right, but if they're late, we're all in trouble, including those people downstream in the process. You know the policy here: two weeks from this oral warning to meet our expectations or I have to put you on written notice. Since the job's such a vital one, I'll be able to give you only two weeks more. Then, if a job exists for you, we'll transfer you; if none exists, I'll have to cut you loose. What do you think?

Mike [*angry*]:   What *can* I think? I've been expecting this. To be hung out on a rope and left dangling. I'm at the wrong place at the wrong time, and I tell you I don't like it!

You: You're feeling angry.

Mike [*snorting, derisive*]:   *Angry* isn't the word for it. Ten years I've given to this company, and this is what it comes down to! Put in a job I'm not qualified to do so you can find cause for firing me!

You: You think we did this deliberately; we set you up.

Mike: Does a duck have webbed feet?

You [*pleasantly*]:   A duck may have them, but I don't. At the same time, I can understand your anger. It must be very frustrating to you.

Mike: You bet it is!

You: How do you see the fact that we gave you a choice between the severance package and a transfer?

Mike: When the downsizing came, my boss said it's because I'm seen as a good soldier and a steady worker. I see it differently: Good soldiers just fade away. They don't cost a lot of money when they quit instead of being fired.

You: Actually, that song says *old* soldiers fade away, and you're right—letting you go would've been more expensive than letting you quit. It still is. So why did the company give you the option and reassign you three times, including to this department?

Mike: Stop jacking me around. You tell me.

You: You think I'm jacking you around.

Mike: Especially with all this active listening stuff you're giving me. I'm calming down, so cut it out. Be straight with me. Why have they spread me around every which way? I'm not over forty, so they're not afraid of a lawsuit.

You: Because you're a good soldier and steady worker, and that kind of solider is hard to find. It'll cost even more to let you go than just the severance package. Mike, you *are* a valued employee—valued for your skills, your knowledge, and your loyalty. You're also a good role model for the younger employees.

Mike [*softly, after a pregnant silence*]: I think you really mean it.

You: I do, but I still have to insist that your layouts get to me on time. This is an oral warning, Jack. What does that mean to you?

Mike: Shape up or ship out.

You: You get more of a chance than that.

Mike: Yeah. Written notice of probation, then ship out.

You: Only if we don't see real improvement. Let's set up an action plan. Maybe we can come up with just the right trick to get you cooking here.

Taking Corrective Action—Written Warning—Angry Employee, Part 2

An oral warning, as step 1, should accomplish its goals. If it doesn't, you have to take step 2: written notice of performance probation. In this event:

1. Set out the problem in terms of the expectations that are not being met and outlining how the employee has failed to meet them.
2. Document the problem with references to previous conversations, memos in the employee's performance management file, and whatever else supports your action.
3. Discuss the situation calmly.
4. Let the employee ventilate feelings.
5. Stay cool, fair, and courteous but determined.

Scenario—Angry Employee, Part 2

Mike still doesn't meet expectations. His layouts have improved, but he's still missing his deadlines, sometimes by as many as two days. You have discussed this next action with the Human Resources Department, received help in writing the memo, and set up a meeting with Jack.

Key Phrases
Communicating Formal Performance Probation

"Your performance level still has not reached acceptable levels."
"We've discussed the situation on several occasions, and. . . ."
"You were given an oral warning, and. . . ."
"If you're not meeting these standards by . . . , we'll have to. . . ."

Mike: Don't waste your breath or time with preliminaries. I'm not meeting my deadlines and you're teed off.

You: I see you're angrier now than you were the last time we met like this.

Mike: I'm much more threatened now. I know you're putting me on probation, and that means my job's on the line. I've checked around, and outside of the mailroom, there's nothing here for me. Next stop's the unemployment line.

You: You're sure it'll come to that?

Mike: Yes, I am. How about you?

You: To be honest, maybe. By the time we reach this point, it's clear that nothing we've done has worked. I know it's not a question of willingness or motivation; it's a matter of skill level. We need a journeyman, and you're an apprentice.

Mike:　Why'd we close down plant development?

You:　That's what's hurting you most, isn't it?

Mike:　I've been a drafter all my life. I'm good at it, too. I know the latest methods, even some we didn't use here. So if I'm fired, I won't stand on that unemployment line very long. I'll probably find another job with one of those firms we're hiring now.

You:　That's what you want?

Mike:　No. I've got an investment here. Let's see your memo.

You:　Here's a copy of it. Read it. We'll talk about it and go from there.

Mike: [*after reading the memo shown in the accompanying box*]:　Covers all the bases.

You [*compassionately*]:　Mike, I think both you and I know that this is the best we can do.

Mike [*exploding*]:　It's just not fair, dammit! I put ten years of my life into this damn company. I was a senior drafter. I had a life here. An investment. That's why I elected to ride it out. You take away my job, and now you boot me out the door.

You [*sincerely*]:　I understand your frustration and anger.

Mike:　How can you? I'm the one getting jacked around.

You [*quietly, matter of factly*]:　I was laid off from a company once too.

Mike [*not hearing*]:　I spent more of my life in this building than I did in my own home. I have more overtime, without comp time, than you've had in years in this company. This is the thanks. Booted out the door!

Sample Memo
Written Warning

TO:　　　　　Jack Smith
SUBJECT:　　Performance Probation
DATE:　　　　August 8, 19xx

Problem

As difficult as it is, I must inform you that your performance hasn't reached the level our department needs. The requirement is that all layouts and paste-up artwork be submitted by the "drop-dead" target date set at the beginning of the project. You often miss your targets (80 percent of the time), not from a lack of desire to do it but from a lack of skill needed. Additionally, I have had to rework your layouts totally on two occasions and have had to redo almost all of them in some way.

Previous Action

We have discussed this situation on several occasions, and two work-weeks ago, you were given an oral warning that unless your performance improved to the point where you were meeting your deadlines at least 90 percent of the time and turning in camera-ready artwork all of the time, we would have to put you on performance probation. I have coached you, the company has paid for extra training for you, and you have made yourself available to as many opportunities for help as you can. We must conclude that, for some reason, you are not able to make the adjustments needed.

Current Action

You are hereby placed on performance probation for two workweeks from this date. If you are not meeting all your deadlines with camera-ready artwork by the end of that time, we will have to transfer you to another area of the company (if a position is available) or terminate your employment with the company.

Action Steps

1. All assignments will be completed by their drop-dead dates.
2. All your paste-ups will be camera ready.
3. I will help you start each assignment, check on your progress each evening, and lend as much assistance as I can.
4. If you are dismissed, you will receive the same severance package you would have received when the first layoffs were announced one year ago.

Added Comments

_____   _____

         Signature   *Signature*

You: It sounds as if you've given up.

Mike: Haven't you?

You [*sincerely*]: No. You're a good man, Mike. I want to give you every chance I can.

Mike: Some chance you're giving me by writing a memo like this for my personnel file.

You [*caringly*]: You're concerned that this memo will hurt your chances for finding another job.

Mike: Damn right.

You: Let's write your concern into the memo. I can promise that only if you don't fulfill the terms of this memo will I let you go, and I can also promise that no one will ever tell a prospective employer anything more than the basic name, rank, and serial number.

Mike [*sarcastically*]: Sure.

You [*emphatically*]: Mike, we wouldn't say anything more than that for even the worst employees we ever had. We don't want to stop anyone from earning a living. If it doesn't work out here, it doesn't mean you can't make it elsewhere. I'll write in my promise on the memo, and you can add any comments you like. Then we can sign it.

Mike: I'm not going to sign that damn thing.

You [*persistently but not harshly*]: You're firm about that.

Mike: Dead on.

You [*matter of factly*]: I have to add that to the comments section—that you refused to sign the memo. Would you initial that comment for me?

Mike: Yes.

You [*friendly*]: I'd like you to tell me why you refuse to sign.

Mike [*after a pregnant silence*]: It's admitting that I can't cut it in this assignment—that I failed. I don't want to admit that.

You: I understand that. It's hard. It really is.

Mike: If it were you, would you sign it?

You [*kindly*]: I can't answer that, but I do understand what you're saying.

Taking Corrective Action—Dismissing An Employee—Angry Employee, Part 3

Any kind of warning is hard to deliver. Letting someone go is even harder. In this situation:

- If reasons must be given, state them in terms of unfulfilled expectations and the employee's failure to meet them.
- Empathize with the employee's feelings.
- Allow the employee an opportunity to ventilate feelings.
- Support the employee's self-esteem.

Scenario—Angry Employee, Part 3

Mike missed two deadlines during the two weeks, and you had to revise three layouts. You have to let Mike go.

Key Phrases
Dismissing an Employee for Poor Performance

"I'm truly sorry that it has come to this."
"I've given you ample warning and opportunities to. . . ."
"We've set fair standards for. . . ."
"We value you as a person."

Mike [*angrily*]:   Don't even say it. I know you're sorry it's come to this, you've given me ample warning, and more opportunities to meet the standards. Yeah, I know the whole spiel.

You: I understand your anger.

Mike: Right. You've been laid off too. But not like this. Not with a bad performance record.

You: You're still concerned about someone hearing about this.

Mike: Wouldn't we be lying to say anything else?

You: I said before that we're letting you go with a decent severance package, and we won't do anything to prevent you from finding another job. We'll help you where we can.

Mike: Great. Two weeks' pay, paid-up insurance for a month, and help writing my resume. That's what I get for ten years of service.

You: We have no alternative, and the severance is better than two weeks' pay. We set fair standards for you, but they seemed to be too much to ask of you. Without the skills or the experience needed in this job, you can't meet the standards. Those are the facts. We value you as a person, and we thought keeping you on in some other capacity would be the best for you and for us. We gave you the choice then, and you declined a severance package. We were all wrong. We see that now. What do you think of what I'm saying?

Mike: It's a pretty speech, but— I'm trying to be fair to you, but I'm too angry to care about how you feel.

You: I can understand that, too, and I'm not taking your anger personally. We'll do everything we can to help you line up another position in architectural drafting. The vice president has already placed some calls to those vendors you said you'd wind up working for.

Mike: I've sent out some feelers. I think I'll land on my feet.

You: I'm convinced you will, Mike. You're a good drafter, a good employee, and a good person. We all wish you well.

Conclusion

Applying objective appraisal methods to everyone's performance makes it easier to document why you put an employee on probation or had to fire him. Even so, you still have to be prepared to deal with heated emotion. Letting the person vent feelings and empathizing with them but being firm in your resolve and supporting the person's self-esteem helps him feel more secure and will often turn around a bad performance situation before reaching the written warning stage.

Chapter 15
Firing Rule Breakers

Most companies have policies—sometimes written, sometimes informal—that management believes are essential to the well-being and safety of the company, all employees, and the public the company serves. They expect managers to enforce the rules and to take swift corrective action when the rules have been violated.

That's what companies want, but often they distribute the rules manual with a memo that says, "Please read." No discussion, no training, no support. Do you know the term *dust collector?* It's a synonym for *policy manual.*

Yet in any social organization, from treehouse club to nation-state, rules define the limits of what members can and cannot do to remain members. They spell out the terms of acceptability and the consequences for failing to follow the rules. Some rules seem more equitable to the members than others, but all rules serve the welfare of the organization, and the organization's welfare should concern its managers.

Communicating the Rules—The Ideal Situation

The demand that managers enforce the rules requires them to:

- Know what the rules say—their intent as well as their content.
- Take ownership of the rules and follow the rules themselves.
- Communicate the rules to their employees, explaining their intent as well as their content, and answering questions to the best of their abilities.

Scenario—The Ideal Situation

The plant's safety committee has published new guidelines based on Occupational Safety and Health Administration (OSHA) regulations that affect the industry. The plant manager put all managers, supervisors, and team leaders through a crash course on the guidelines, and for the most part they make sense—especially since the plant's accident rate rose last year. No one protested the rules because they know that unless everyone follows them, lives can be endangered. The day after the meeting on the new guidelines, you call a department safety meeting, distribute the new guidelines, and discuss them one at a time.

Key Phrases
Counseling for Inappropriate Behavior

"The policy states that, in order to [preserve order/protect safety/ etc.]. . . ."

"I believe it's important for me to enforce this policy because. . . ."

"When you [act in a specific way], you violate the policy and [disrupt the workplace/jeopardize safety]."

"Since [a specific behavior] has jeopardized . . . , I will have to terminate your employment immediately."

"I want you to [alter a specific behavior in a given time frame] or I'll have to give you a written warning and place you on disciplinary probation if it happens again."

"You've been told what we expect and you've been given oral and written warnings, but since the [specific behavior] has continued, I have to terminate your employment immediately."

You: So, I've gone over all the new rules. What questions do you still have about them, or about the older guidelines we've retained? [*After a minute of paper rustling and murmuring:*] These rules make sense, and I back them 100 percent. I'd rather be called a hard-nosed SOB than see any one of you hurt or killed. So I intend to enforce them all.

Chris: This rule about "face hair." It looks as if it means I have to shave off my beard.

You: What does the rule say?

Chris: "Face hair that interferes with the proper wearing of breathing apparatus has to be removed or trimmed in a manner that permits the breathing apparatus to fit snugly to the face, particularly around the chin and neck."

You: Does that mean you have to shave off your beard?

Chris: If I don't, the breathing apparatus won't fit properly.

You: Several of you other men have face hair. If you want, we'll meet when this meeting is over and talk about it. Any other discussion? [*When no one speaks up:*] Okay. Let's get to work.

Counseling in Relation to the Rules—Rebellious Employee, Part 1

Be prepared to tolerate dissent when you open rules to discussion or dialog, but if the rules aren't subject to change, candor is the best policy. You should also:

- Apply the rules evenhandedly and fairly.
- Consider exceptions only on the merits of the situation and only in consultation with the head enforcement person or group in the organization (e.g., vice president of human resources).
- When counseling an employee in violation of a rule, spell out the rule and compare the employee's behavior to it.

Scenario—Rebellious Employee, Part 1

Chris, the bearded man who spoke up during the meeting, is the only one to stay behind to discuss the rules. He is outspoken but a good worker. He came to work for you from another department where he reportedly argued frequently with his supervisor, a grizzled veteran of the plants who tolerated no arguments (even if the employees were right). So far, you and Chris have had a few disagreements, but they've all been constructive. This time you aren't so sure about how constructive the discussion will be.

Key Phrases
Counseling for Rules Violations

"What do you think the rule says?"
"Why do you think we think the rule is important or necessary?"
"What alternative do you think we have?"
"How can we accommodate both your needs and ours, and still obey the rule?"

Chris: I think the rule's a crock.

You: Why?

Chris: When's the last time we had a red alert [disaster drill alarm]?

You: We've never had one, but what difference does that make?

Chris: The chances of contaminants' polluting the air and killing us are a million to one. Shaving off my beard for lopsided odds like that doesn't make sense.

You: Have you a medical reason for wearing your beard?

Chris: You mean like Richard? What's that skin problem black guys have?

You: Pseudofolliculitis barbae. I know that only because Richard has it, and the safety committee had to deal with it when it came up with these guidelines.

Chris: I'm surprised he isn't here protesting too.

You: Should he protest?

Chris: He's got face hair.

You: That's his issue, not yours. Let's talk about yours.

Chris: If he doesn't shave off his, why should I? If the women don't have to cut their hair short, why should I shave off my beard? Let's look at the fairness of this.

You: You wear a beard because . . . ?

Chris: I like a beard.

You: Not for a religious or medical reason?

Chris: No.

You: And you think the policy requires you to shave off the beard.

Chris: Doesn't it?

You: It says that you can trim it to accommodate the breathing mask. I don't think the rule is open to change. The OSHA committee even took the trouble to have a model's beard trimmed and photographed to show how you can do that.

Chris: Yeah. I saw it. It looks pretty dumb to me. I think the rule's a crock, and I don't intend to shave my beard.

You: During the drill last week, did you try on the mask?

Chris: Yeah.

You: What happened?

Chris: It fit, sorta. It was a little loose around the chin, but I still think the odds that we'll ever need it are too slim to make it worth shaving off my beard.

You: Chris, I've heard you out; I've explained the rule and its intent. Now I have to enforce it. Consider this to be your oral warning. Shave it off or trim it by tomorrow, or we'll have to take steps to dismiss you for failure to comply with an important safety rule designed to protect your life. If you comply, no further action will be taken, and this whole incident will be forgotten.

Warnings of Corrective Action—Rebellious Employee, Part 2

Once you decide to enforce a rule, idle threats undermine both your authority and the rule. You must:

1. Take firm, immediate action if the employee's behavior jeopardizes his own safety or that of other people, endangers the organization's mission, or endangers the welfare of the public that the organization serves.
2. Follow the guidelines for progressive disciplinary action: oral warning, then written warning (including terms of disciplinary probation), then dismissal.

Scenario—Rebellious Employee, Part 2

The morning after the first conversation about the beard, Chris returns to work still unshaven. You have to give an oral warning.

Key Phrases
Oral Warning of Corrective Action

"Even though I gave you fair warning, I see you're still. . . ."
"The rule is designed to . . . , and it has to be enforced."
"Here is why I insist that we all follow this rule. . . ."
"You can file a [complaint/grievance], but I still will. . . ."

You: Chris, you haven't removed or trimmed your beard in accordance with the new safety guidelines.

Chris: I said I wouldn't. The rule is a crock.

You: I disagree. The rule is designed for your personal safety. I too doubt that we'll have a red alert in our lifetime, only because we're following all the right safety rules, but you never know what could happen. Look at South St. Louis during the floods of '93. Those Phillips butane tanks tore loose and endangered thousands of lives. A natural disaster could do the same to us. A tornado that hits one of those storage tanks, lightning that sets fire to a generator that blows up a fuel line, or any number of freak accidents might force us into a red alert. Everyone else will put on breathing equipment and live. You'll put it on and die.

Chris: Scare tactics are beneath you. What about Richard and the women with long hair?

You: Richard trimmed his beard. The women's hair is regulation length.

Chris: Well, good for them.

You: I need to know if you understand our reasoning. It's one thing if you're rebelling for rebellion's sake, but it's another if we haven't made ourselves clear.

Chris: Yeah. I understand it. You think a red alert's possible—maybe not probable, but possible. The rule was written because the way the new breathing masks fit under our chins and around our necks. My beard could get in the way and leave room for poisoned air to leak under the mask.

You: Well, since you understand the rule, I can only conclude you're insubordinate without proper cause. I could dismiss you on the spot for this, but, Chris, to be fair, I want to give you more time to think about it. I want you to talk with Human Resources about it too. You can file a complaint about me and the rule; it's your right. Or talk with the chairperson of the safety committee. But I'm going to make this notice official with a written warning. As of this moment, I'm placing you under disciplinary probation. Ordinarily I have the leeway to give a person two workweeks to comply, but because of the safety risk involved, I'm giving you only two extra days. If you haven't trimmed your beard or removed it by the day after tomorrow, I'll have to terminate your employment without severance pay or other benefits. You'll have the written memo to sign within the hour.

Sample Memo
Disciplinary Written Warning

TO: Chris Jones
SUBJECT: Disciplinary Probation for Violating Safety Code III.3
DATE: August 10, 19xx

Safety Code Violation

Safety Code III.3: "Face hair that interferes with the proper wearing of breathing apparatus has to be removed or trimmed in a manner that permits the breathing apparatus to fit snugly to the face, particularly around the chin and neck." You have refused to comply with this regulation, and your insubordination puts your own life in danger, an action that this company cannot accept.

Previous Action

A department meeting was held in which the new safety rules were read and discussed. You objected to this rule during the meeting, and

I gave you and other interested parties an opportunity to discuss the rule with me. Only you stayed behind to discuss the rule, and you refused during that meeting to comply. I gave you an oral warning on the spot and overnight to comply. This morning you returned to work without trimming or removing your beard. You refused again. I have made an appointment for you to discuss this with the Human Resources Department and with the chairperson of the safety committee (4:30 P.M., August 10, 19xx). I have also given you two workdays to comply (by August 12, 19xx).

Consequences for Failure to Comply

Should you not comply by August 12, 19xx, unless I am overruled by a higher authority, I will immediately terminate your employment with this company without severance pay or benefits. If you do comply, the matter will be dropped without further discussion or comment. However, this memo will be put on file until after your annual appraisal is written, and if you allow your beard to grow back in a manner that interferes with the breathing apparatus, I will terminate your employment immediately.

Comments

_____   _____
             Signature   *Signature*

Dismissing an Employee for Disciplinary Reasons—Rebellious (and, Now, Angry) Employee, Part 3

When you write a formal probation notice, abide by its terms if you expect the other person to do so. Give the person the opportunity spelled out in the memo, and follow through on whatever consequences you described. When terminating an employee's employment for rules violations:

- Make clear the rules violations.
- Review the steps taken to date.
- Let the employee ventilate if necessary.

Scenario—Rebellious (and, Now, Angry) Employee, Part 3

Chris refuses to shave off or trim his face hair, in spite of the warnings he has received.

Key Phrases
Dismissing an Employee for Violations of Rules

"In spite of all the warnings, you still. . . . "
"I'm left with no other alternative than to terminate your employment."
"You have . . . to put matters in order before leaving."
"These are the terms of your termination: . . ."

You: You've talked with Human Resources and with the safety committee. We've talked about it, and I've given you a written warning that you signed. You still haven't trimmed or removed your beard in compliance with Safety Code III.3.

Chris: I don't think it's necessary, and I won't do it. I have the right to dress or keep my appearance to my own taste as long as I'm not endangering anyone else. I talked with an attorney about this last night.

You: What do you intend to do?

Chris: I don't know yet. I only know that I won't remove or trim this beard, and you're going to fire me this morning. Right?

You: Right.

Chris: Then do it.

You: It's done. I'll process the paperwork immediately. Remove your gear from your locker. A security guard is waiting to accompany you. Leave all company property where it is.

Chris: I have personal tools at my workstation.

You: Clearly identified?

Chris [*angrily*]: You think I'd steal your damn tools?

You: The security guard will have to separate them, that's all.

Chris [*angrily*]: You really have turned on me.

You: You feel I'm treating you unfairly.

Chris [*angrily*]: I'm not going to take this sitting down. You've thrown me out of here, taken my livelihood away, and made a federal case out of a minor thing. You're damn right I think it's unfair. [*After a pregnant silence:*] Why shouldn't I protest? We got along just fine without that breathing equipment. We don't even need it. Now I'm fired because some damn piece of equipment is more important than I am. If this were a union shop, you wouldn't get away with it.

You: I understand your anger. That's why I made it possible for you to use our grievance process. You presented your case to Human Resources and to the safety committee, and no one agreed with you. If you were to talk to the general manager, you'd hear him roar. I'm sure you've talked about this with the men on the shop floor.

Chris: I have.

You [*after it's clear that Chris isn't saying more*]: I don't know what they said to you, but those I've spoken to think it's a good rule— even the men with face hair in other departments.

Chris [*a little more subdued*]: It's my beard and my right, not theirs that I care about.

You: Chris, this conversation is getting us nowhere. I'm not down on you, and I won't do anything to interfere with your application for employment at any other company. I appreciate your position, but I don't agree with it. Termination is effective immediately. You'll receive a check for your last two weeks of work in the mail. I wish you the best of luck.

Conclusion

Managers have to protect the welfare of the organization, its employees, and the public it serves. That doesn't mean that managers can never question policies or procedures, but the place in which they do it is in their own managers' offices. At the same time, until they can create the change they think appropriate, they have to own the rules, be committed to them, apply them equally and fairly, and enforce them—firmly when necessary.

Chapter 16

Implementing The Decision to Downsize

It's tough to fire someone whose performance doesn't meet standards or whose behavior is unacceptable. It's tougher still to lay off people because a business decision has been made to eliminate their jobs. It's also tough to manage the people who remain behind—the survivors.

Downsizing affects everyone directly, immediately, and traumatically. Everyone who is severed experiences the shock of having to find work. The first jolt to their self-esteem comes from losing their jobs. The second jolt comes when they find out how difficult it is to replace their jobs in a swollen, highly competitive labor market. It isn't easy for them, and it isn't easy for you to break the news.

Nothing can really soften the blow when you let people go. They'll go through stages that range from denial to anger to acceptance. They'll resent you and the people who stay behind. They'll feel sorry for themselves. They'll seek sympathy from everyone. The best you can do for them is to help them leave gracefully and be as empathetic as possible.

The survivors face different traumas, from *retaining* their jobs. They wind up having to do the work of many with fewer resources. My own experience with downsizing companies is that little thought is given to how to manage the survivors. Too often managers tell the remaining few that they should feel fortunate that they haven't been laid off too. The employees interpret that as a threat: "Toe the line or hit the road." Those managers seem not to have ever heard that their most important customers are their employees.

Communicating major changes to individuals and to groups always affects how well employees do on the job. A recent study, reported in the *Wall Street Journal* (September 3, 1993), makes it clear that "open communication" is the number one reason behind employees' decisions to take the job they are in. That same study showed the next five top rankings of what is important to employees:

1. The job's effect on family or personal life
2. The nature of the work
3. Management quality
4. The supervisor
5. Control over the content of the work

Wage and salary ranked only sixteenth out of twenty reasons for making a job decision.

Especially when a company is reorganized, managers who talk to employees, keep them informed, listen to their ideas and opinions, and recognize what is important to them will get the highest level of performance from staff. Clearly every manager must make a strong effort to connect with their subordinates.

All changes carry risks and burdens with them. Certainly change is constant, but people usually see it as something that happens to them suddenly rather than something that goes on all the time or that they can initiate or manage. The feeling that change happens to them creates resistance, fear of the unknown (which then creates more resistance), and a form of inertia that idealizes the past and struggles to maintain the status quo—all in vain.

The failure to communicate with and involve employees contributes to the fact that few companies benefit from downsizing in the short run. Several different analysts writing in the *Wall Street Journal* in 1993 have estimated that barely 30 percent of the companies that have reduced their workforce over the past four or five years have succeeded in greatly improving their profitability. Why? The reason, in part, is that the survivors aren't as productive as they were or as the full complement of employees had been.

You can reduce the initial resistance to change in general by involving those who are affected in the initial stages of a consciously induced change. Encourage them not only to participate but also to see what's in it for them to join in the transition and make things happen that benefit them as well as the organization. Working with the survivors of a reduction in force (RIF) almost cries out for participative problem solving. How are we going to manage the transition, and how are we going to handle the workload?

Laying Off Valuable Employees—Telling An Employee She Is Being Let Go

The organization can do a lot to help laid-off employees and the survivors, and so can individual managers. The process begins with compassion. When laying off employees:

- Make a concerted effort to recognize and respect their dignity. Give them fair notice, a decent severance package, and help in finding a new job.
- Speak with them in a tone of regret rather than with indifference or matter-of-factness; show concern.
- Personally offer to help laid-off employees in whatever ways you can, given company policies.
- Show concern and give guidance, not sympathy.
- Provide laid-off employees with opportunities to vent their feelings.

Scenario—Telling an Employee She Is Being Let Go

When three major hospitals in the one county merged, certain staff positions were considered redundant, especially positions in human resources. The first units to feel the axe's sharp blade in all three hospitals were the training and education groups: a 40 percent across-the-board reduction was ordered.

Billie, the manager of the largest unit, had the least seniority, having been hired in from the outside one year earlier. The other two managers had been in their positions for several years each, and they would stay to manage more people than they had managed before as a result of merging the survivors of Billie's unit into theirs. No one was happy with the plan, but management decreed the changes and accepted no alternatives. You, the vice president of human resources, have to break the news to Billie: She has to lay off 40 percent of her group—including herself.

Key Phrases
Laying Off an Employee

"It makes me sad to tell you. . . ."

"I wish it could be different, but. . . ."

"It's hard for me to tell you this, but I imagine it's harder for you to hear it."

"Talk to me about your feelings. I can't do much to help the situation, but I can listen and understand."

"Let me see who I know who might help. . . ."

You: I don't know any way of telling you this but honestly and directly. It's hard for me, but everything we've feared has come to pass. The RIF is taking 40 percent out of Human Resources—across the board.

Billie: That's quite a bite. I guess we're now expected to identify who's to go and who's to stay.

You: That's partly right. You have to give me a list by tomorrow morning. And, Billie, this is the hardest part for me. I have to ask you to put your own name on that list. I'm sorry, but we're going to have only two managers from the merger, and you have the least seniority. Erica will head up nurse training and education, and Andy will head up management education and organizational development.

Billie [*after a pregnant silence*]:   I suppose I expected it.

You: I'm sorry, Billie. I hired you because I consider you among the best there is in the management education business. I hate letting you go. If there's anything I can do within the limits I have, please let me do it.

Billie [*resigned but clearly not happy*]:   Sure. Sure thing. [*After a slight pause:*] I guess I'd better go make up my RIF list for you.

Laying Off Valuable Employees—Listening To An Angry Employee

As the initial shock of being laid off fades, employees often let their real feelings hang out, and they often make you the target of their anger. In this situation:

- Encourage employees to ventilate, but be aware of the possibility that some people can become violent.
- Listen for anger that might get out of hand.
- Be supportive without making promises you can't keep.

Scenario—Listening to an Angry Employee

Billie took the news stoically at first. She did what she had to do, but when she returned several days later, she unloaded all that she thought and felt.

Key Phrases
Responding to an Angry Laid-Off Employee

"Tell me what you're feeling."
"What kind of plan have you set up for yourself?"
"What can I do to help you pull together some resources?"
"What do you think the company can do that it's not doing?"

Billie: The whole deal stinks! The demand for training and education will go up, not down. Fewer people to do more work with fewer resources. The nurses are already complaining about the agency help they're getting. Some of those people can't tell the difference between a sputum pan and a bedpan. And this idea of putting rolling X-ray machines and technicians on the floor? I'd rather have a technician standing around with his finger up his nose than trying to help the nurses—until they get the proper training. Nine-week wonders in the army—the corpsmen—have better training than some of the people we've got now. And with this RIF, it'll only get worse.

You: You're quite angry.

Billie: You think *I'm* angry! You should hear some of my people. You try to explain to Pat why our unit is cut by 40 percent while the other two units are merged to do more with less. You want to hear anger? That was anger. You know Pat's temper as well as I do. I put the employee assistance program phone number on the table.

You: Pat's not here. It's your anger I see.

Billie: Hell, yes, I'm angry. I gave up a good job and moved to this city just to head this department. One year later—poof! It's gone.

You: So tell me everything you're feeling.

Billie: You lied to me. You said that the department will grow, even-tually split into three units, each with its own manager. That would give me a shot at becoming a senior manager—a vice president. It was all a lie.

You: You think I deliberately misled you?

Billie: Yes, you did. The only thing that keeps this from becoming a complete disaster is that my youngest child just got a job at a fast food place down the street. We still have family income. He's looking to see if they've got a job for me too.

You: What else are you feeling?

Billie: Besides rage and betrayal? What's left? [*After a slight pause; softer, with a touch of self-pity:*] I trusted you. I believed what you said. I believed in the plan you used to lure me here. How could you stab me in the back like that?

You: What can I tell you that would make you believe that the plan was no lie? It came apart less than a month ago, when the merger went through.

Billie: How long was that merger in the making? It didn't just happen.

You: It was made public three months ago. Until then, no one at my level even knew anyone was talking about it. I don't know whose idea it was, but it's seen as a major step toward reducing unnec-essary duplication of services and providing better care for the patients and better service to the community. That's why the local governments and the state board approved the plan so quickly. I never lied to you, Billie. I've always told you the truth. I didn't expect this to happen, and I truly hoped that your department would be the keystone of training and education when the merger took place.

Billie: So why didn't it happen that way?

You: The budget won't carry it. The whole Human Resources budget got gored and is bleeding to death. [*After a slight pause:*] How do you feel about your severance package?

Billie: Talk about bleeding to death. That package severed an artery. Training jobs have dried up—or haven't you noticed?

You: Yes, I've seen that.

Billie: I'm not an RN, like the other two managers. I have few salable skills other than training and training management.

You: What plans are you making for finding another job?

Billie: None yet. That so-called outplacement service the hospital district hired better have some pretty good ideas for me, or I'm dead in the water.

You: What can I do?

Billie: You? What you always do. Nothing. [*After a pregnant silence:*] No. That's not fair. You've tried. I'm sorry. I guess I am overwrought. Thanks for offering, but the only help I think I need is your network of people you know who need a damn good training manager. I'm available.

Helping the Survivors—Enlisting the Help of An Angry Survivor

Getting the commitment of survivors may be more difficult than it seems. To win their support:

- Avoid exhortation and sloganeering.
- Express regret and concern for the burdens everyone has to bear.
- Be supportive.
- Solicit ideas as to how to reorganize the workload.

- Create a task force to offer alternative models for change.
- Listen to all reasonable suggestions, and implement every workable idea.
- Create a transition team to manage the change.

Scenario—Enlisting the Help of an Angry Survivor

Erica has been with Community Hospital, the smallest of the three hospitals in the merger, for nearly twelve years. During the first eight, she served as a nurse and nursing supervisor; during the last four, she headed the hospital's nurse training and education unit. Until now, the unit had been a two-person show: Erica and a training coordinator. They hadn't needed more than that. Their main activity was continuing education for nurses. Now her job is to head up nurse's aide training, continuing education for nurses, nursing supervision, med-tech training, and "duties as assigned"—and with only one additional person, Andy, to do all that. The mandate is for *more* training with *fewer* personnel and *less* budget. And everyone seems surprised to hear that Erica's angry.

Key Phrases
Winning Support from Angry Survivors

"I understand your feelings."
"I hear what you're saying."
"What suggestions do you have for handling this?"
"I have some ideas I'd like to discuss with you that might help."
"Let's bring in some more people to handle the planning process."
"I think a transition team is in order."

Erica [*angrily*]:   This is the worst situation I've ever seen! And the only thing our administrator had to say about it was, "Just be glad you still have a job." Just what's that supposed to mean?

You: How did that sound to you, Erica?

Erica: Like a threat.

You: I don't understand.

Erica: "Do what you're told, do it well—and keep your mouth shut. We can do anything we want, and if you don't like it, that's tough."

You: Would it do any good to say that that's not how anyone in management thinks or feels?

Erica: No, because I think you're wrong. *You* may not feel that way but our administrator does. I'm not the only one he's said that to. [*After a slight pause:*] I'm an RN—a damn good charge nurse. I don't need that kind of talk from anyone. The demand for nurses may be drying up but not for nursing supervisors.

You: Erica, that sounds like a threat to me.

Erica: It *is* a threat, by damn! If you fire me or I quit, you can rehire Billie.

You: Is that what you want?

Erica [*after a pause*]: No. But I want some consideration for what has to be done here, with the budget cut and the head count reduced. Merging facilities and equipment makes good fiscal sense for the hospitals, but it doesn't do anything for the troops.

You: What do you want to see happen?

Erica: More time, more support.

You: You have some ideas on how to go about this?

Erica: I wish I did. I feel swamped. I really do.

You: Erica, I hear what you're saying. This whole process is tough on everyone, and I feel much the same way you do: swamped. I lost 40 percent of my staff in one day. I need time and support too. I need it from you and from Pat and Andy and from everyone else, as well as from upper management. I have an idea that may make it easier for everyone. Interested?

Erica: I'll listen to anything that might make things easier. Shoot.

You: Your workload has grown four times as big. So has Andy's. You two managers hardly know each other, and your staffs don't know one another at all. If you work together to come up with a coordinated training and education plan, you could give each other the time and support you need. I'm doing everything I can to get more support for the whole human resources effort, but

I'm making a special effort for you. Training will become more important now than ever. Billie was right about that. Unless we spin up your efforts, quality of care will go down.

Erica: It sounds good in here, but how does it fly in the boardroom?

You: You're the first person I've spoken to about it except for the chief administrator. She's behind my entire plan, and she's pulling money out of her contingency funds to help. She has also been talking to your administrator and Andy's. They've expressed some reluctance about the management development effort—the so-called soft skills—but they've come to see the importance to quality of the whole team approach to training.

Erica: So, give. What's the plan?

You: I'd like to see everyone from training and education come together as a task force at a facilitated retreat. I'll be the facilitator. As a group, you'll do the strategic thinking and come up with a two-year plan that includes the sharing of resources and personnel. We have your budget allowances for the two years. You create a transition team to implement the plan. It'll be your plan—and your responsibility and authority to execute it.

Erica: A retreat and a transition team. She's got the money for that but not for additional people?

You: Give me a chance. Give my idea a few minutes to gel in your mind. As for the money, I'm trying to get the facilities for free, so it'll cost us only for food and transportation. We couldn't hire anyone for two days for that kind of money.

Erica: I'm sorry. I'm still feeling burned.

You: I understand your feelings, and you'll never hear it from me that you should be glad to have a job. It's much harder for us now than it has ever been, and I can't say that we're all that fortunate. Yet there's a point to this. We can make something of this change if we work together to our own benefit, as well as to the hospital's. Give it a chance.

Erica: Sure. I know what you're saying. So, let's. . . .

Conclusion

What you said in that last dialog bears repeating: "We can make something of this change if we work together to our own benefit, as well as to the hospital's." You didn't say, "Let's make the best of it," which is somewhat negative. Doing something for your own benefit makes a bitter change easier to take.

My mother used to say, "Everything happens for the best." I didn't agree with that then, and I still don't. Things happen for the best *only* if you make them happen for the best. Much of your destiny is in your own hands, but you have to reach out to grasp it.

Epilogue

Some Final Words About Management Style

Here is one last dialog, a conversation between you and me. The style of management set out in this book reflects my personal bias for participative and active management. Perhaps I can answer some questions you have and tie up some loose ends as well.

You: Throughout the book, you seem to say that I should ask a whole lot of questions. Since I'm the manager, why not just tell people what to do and when to do it?

Don: And how high to jump? No, that's just a joke. Management in the past did just that. We call it command-and-control management. It worked for most managers in another industrial era, at another time, and with employees used to taking orders. Most of today's workforce isn't like that. They've come to expect much better treatment than their parents received from management.

You: Better treatment? (There I go again, asking still another question.)

Don: They want stimulating work, control over their worklife. The buzz word for the nineties is *empowerment*. And most of all, they want to be heard. So listen to them. The best way to listen is to ask a question and shut up.

You: You're asking a whole lot from me. Sometimes it seems you suggest that I become Mary Poppins, Miss Goody-Two-Shoes, and Pollyanna all smushed into one beleaguered, overworked, underpaid manager. Nobody can be that good. Well, maybe Mother Teresa can, but not me.

Don: No one said quality management is easy. Sometimes for the sake of creating a productive environment, you have to swallow your tongue until you can find a way to say what's on your mind without coming down harshly on other people. I never say to lie, to sandbag your opinions, or to hide your feelings. I suggest only that you express yourself in a way that recognizes the dignity of the other person and gives her the respect you feel is due you.

You: I get the feeling that other people will see this kind of management as weakness, as indecisive—in fact, not capable of making a decision.

Don: Some people will see this style as weakness. Employees don't automatically adjust to the style any more than do managers. I'll make two points here. First, managers have to be trained to become tough minded yet open minded. Second, employees have to be trained to respond to this kind of management.

You: Tough-minded open-mindedness. That sounds like an oxymoron.

Don: Consider how you handled Jason in the sexual harassment scenario and Fred when he was missing deadlines. You had objectives to achieve, and you achieved them, but at the same time, you left the door open to getting the results you wanted through means your employees suggested. You fired Jason. You turned Fred's attitudes around. These are hardly signs of weakness.

You: It can't happen overnight.

Don: I agree. It can't. Not even after reading this book. You need training and practice to make it happen. You need team leadership training, especially on how to facilitate group decision making that makes it clear that you have a mind of your own but that you recognize that everyone else has one too. I recommend that you make decisions, that you be decisive, but that you listen to the people whom you're asking to carry out your decisions. They have the experience and the talent you need to make effective decisions that will produce the results you want.

You: How do you train employees to accept this?

Don: Encourage team efforts where and when you can: safety, work distribution, work flow, cost savings, production needs. Those considerations have a direct effect on the work lives of the employees and lend themselves to teamwork efforts.

You: You're saying then that labor-management cooperation is the in thing.

Don: Not yet, but it's the coming thing. The scripts I've written all reflect that type of thinking. They stop short of calling for self-directed management in which managers don't play an important role managing the group, but they do lend themselves to developing more autonomy for all employees.

Index

action plan, 31–32
  coaching employees and, 94–95,
    105, 109–110
  competitive peers and, 160
  description of, 7–8
  disagreeing with the boss and,
    14–15
  judgmental behavior and,
    128–129
  shy employees and, 123
active and participative manage-
    ment, 201–203
age discrimination, 131–133
appraising employee performance,
    75–76
  formally, 77–78, 83–89
  informally, 77–83
assertiveness and feedback, 18

benefit packages, 63–64, 71
benefit statements, 17, 18
boss
  building a relationship with the,
    160–162
  disagreeing with the action plan
    and, 14–15
  exchange stage and, 9–12
  openers stage and, 8–9
  resolution of differences with,
    12–13

building relationships
  with boss everyone resents,
    160–162
  with competitive peers, 157–160
  with employees suspicious of
    your motives, 153–157

"chemistry" and hiring decisions,
    50
coaching employees, 75–76, 100
  with defensive tendencies, 95–98
  into leadership positions,
    101–111
  performance improvement and,
    95–99
  techniques for successfully,
    90–95
collaborating on writing formal ap-
    praisal, 83–89
committee approach to interview-
    ing, 49
communication
  difficult employees and, 115–123
  downsizing and, 190–191
  effective, 7–15
  of rules, 178–180
competitive peers, 157–160
consequences and feedback, 16, 18
corrective action, 165–166
  firing employees, 176–177,
    185–187
  oral warning, 166–171

corrective action (*continued*)
  problem solving and, 33–34
  rule enforcement, 178–187
  written warning, 171–175
corrective feedback, 40–43, 80–83
counseling in relation to the rules,
  180–182

data collection, 25–26
defensive employees, 18–22, 95–98
differences between employees
  age discrimination and, 131–133
  judgmental behavior and,
    124–129
  minorities and, 129–131
  sexual harassment and, 133–136
difficult employees, 113–116
  know-it-alls, 117–120
  shy people, 120–123
disabled individuals, 63
disagreeing with the boss
  action plan and, 14–15
  exchange stage and, 9–12
  openers stage and, 8–9
  resolution of differences and,
    12–13
disciplining employees, *see* correc-
    tive action
discrimination
  age, 131–133
  against Jews, 129–131
  sexual, 133–136, 139–152
discussion management, 5
  communicating effectively and,
    7–15
  encouraging employees and,
    35–48
  feedback and, 16–22
  problem solving and, 23–34
documentation of performance
    problems, 166
downsizing decisions, 189–191

listening to angry employees
    about, 193–195
  survivors of, enlisting help of,
    195–198
  telling employees about, 191–192

educational history and hiring de-
    cisions, 49–50
80/20 rule, 26, 54
either/or questions, 54
emotional issues, 35
employee handbook, 66, 70–71
employees
  communicating effectively with,
    7–15
  corrective action and, 165–187
  difficult, 115–123
  encouraging, 35–44
  feedback to, 4, 16–22, 40–43, 78–
    83, 96
  harassment claims of, 62, 71, 114,
    137–152
  interviewing prospective, 47–65
  laying off, 189–198
  managing differences between,
    124–126
  orientating new, 66–73
  performance management of,
    75–110
  problem solving with, 23–34
  relationship building between,
    153–162
encouraging employees, 35–36,
    44–45
  through corrective feedback,
    40–43
  downsizing decisions and,
    190–191
  by listening well, 38–40
  techniques for, 36–37
equal employment opportunity
    laws, 47, 62, 137

exchange stage in discussion, 7
building relationships with employees and, 155–156
coaching employees and, 92–93, 96–97, 102–104, 107–108
competitive peers and, 158–159
corrective feedback and, 41–43
disagreeing with the boss and, 9–12
feedback and, 17
formal appraisal and, 86–87
inexperienced workers and, 70–72
informal appraisal and, 82–83
interviewing prospective employees and, 55–56, 57–59
judgmental behavior and, 126–127
oral warning and, 170–171
reassuring new employees and, 68–69
shy employees and, 121–122

Fair, Square, and Legal (Weiss), 3, 47, 136, 137
family background and hiring decisions, 50
feedback, 16–18, 96
defensive employees and, 18–22
encouraging employees through corrective, 40–43
informal appraisal and, 78–83
practicing, 4
feelings
mirroring/reflecting, 18, 20, 21, 36, 39, 44–45, 91, 96, 97, 98
negative, 35
Fifth Discipline, The (Senge), 75
firing employees
key phrases for, 179
for poor performance, 176–177
rules violations and, 185–187

formal appraisals, 77–78, 83–89

goals/objectives/standards, measurable, 77
growth and development, coaching for, 100–111

handbook for new employees, 66, 70–71
harassment claims, 62, 71, 114, 137–139
see also sexual harassment
health care coverage, 63–64
hiring employees, *see* interviewing prospective employees
history of employees and hiring decisions, 49–50
hostile environment
building relationships within, 153–162
communicating with difficult people in, 115–123
differences between people causing, 124–136
harassment claims causing, 137–152

identifying problems, 24–28
implementing plans in problem solving, 31–32
inexperienced workers and orientation procedures, 69–73
informal appraisals, 77–83
information, probing for, 10, 54
interviewing prospective employees, 49–50
questions asked when, 52–56
second interview, 56–59
shy applicants, 50–53
for supervisory positions, 60–65
I-statements, 18, 19, 22

Jewish employees, 129–131
job description, 51, 67, 72–73, 89
job experience and orientation procedures, 69–73
judgmental behavior, 124–129

key phrases for
  action planning, 14
  appraisal language, 79, 81, 85, 86
  building relationships, 154, 161
  coaching employees, 92, 96, 102, 106
  competitive peers, dealing with, 158
  corrective feedback, 41
  counseling for rules violations, 181
  differences between people, 126
  80/20 rule, 26
  encouraging employees, 43–44
  feedback, giving, 17
  firing employees, 176–177, 179, 186
  harassing others, confronting someone about, 134
  identifying real problems, 24
  interviewing prospective employees, 52, 57, 60, 62
  I-statements, 19
  know-it-all employees, 118
  laying off employees, 192, 193
  mirroring feelings, 39
  open-ended questions, 37
  oral warnings, 167–168, 183
  orientation of new employees, 68, 69
  probationary procedures, 172
  probing for information, 10, 54
  problem solving alternatives, 29
  resolving differences, 12
  sexual harassment charges, probing, 139, 149–150
  silence barrier, breaking, 121
  survivors of downsizing, 196
  tentative plans, 31
  unfair/illegal treatment, confronting, 132
  unkind remarks, responding to, 130
know-it-all employees, 117–120

Law of Productive Nothingness, 37
laws pertaining to workplace
  corrective action and, 76
  harassment claims and, 136, 137, 144–145
  interviewing prospective employees and, 47, 62
laying off valuable employees, 191–195
leadership positions, coaching employees into, 101–111
learning organization, 75, 110–111
listening well to encourage employees, 26, 38–40, 54, 193–195

management style, 201–203
managing discussions effectively, 5, 7–15
measurable goals/objectives/standards, 77
minority employees, 61, 63, 129–131
mirroring feelings
  coaching employees and, 91, 96, 97, 98
  encouraging employees and, 36, 39, 44–45
  feedback and, 18, 20, 21
monitoring plans when problem solving, 32–33

needs recognition and feedback, 18–19

negative feedback, 40–43, 80–83
negative feelings, 35

objective appraisal language, 79
observable goals/objectives/standards, 77
open-ended questions (gatekeepers)
  encouraging employees using, 36, 37, 44
  identifying real problems using, 25–26
  interviewing prospective employees using, 54
  probing for information using, 10
openers stage in discussion, 7, 8–9
  building relationships with employees and, 154–155
  coaching employees and, 92, 96, 102, 106–107
  feedback and, 17
  inexperienced workers and, 70
  informal appraisal and, 82
  interviewing prospective employees and, 55, 57
  reassuring new employees and, 68
oral warnings
  for disciplinary reasons, 183
  to improve job performance, 166–171
orientation of new employees, 66
  inexperienced workers and, 69–73
  probationary procedures and, 166
  using reassurance during, 67–69

paraphrasing, 18, 20, 21, 36
participative and active management, 201–203
pay raises, 64, 72
performance bonus, 88

performance management
  appraising employee performance and, 75–89
  coaching employees and, 90–111
  oral warnings and, 166–171
  written warnings and, 171–175
positive climate, 45
positive feedback, 78–80
pregnant silence, 4, 37
probationary procedures, 166, 171–175, 184
probing for information, 10, 54
problem solving, 23
  corrective action when, 33–34
  identifying real problems when, 24–28
  implementing plans when, 31–32
  monitoring plans when, 32–33
  sifting through possibilities when, 28–30
  tentative plans when, 30–31
promises to new employees, 67
promotion policies, 64–65, 71–72
psychological contract, 67–73

questions
  controlling dialog through, 4
  harassment investigation and, 114
  in interviews of prospective employees, 52–56, 62
  see also open-ended questions (gatekeepers)

rapport with new employees, 73
reassuring new employees, 67–69
rebellious employees, 180–187
records of employee performance, 166
reflecting feelings
  coaching employees and, 91, 96, 97, 98
  encouraging employees and, 36, 39, 44–45
  feedback and, 18, 20, 21

relationships, managing, 113–115
  by building relationships,
    153–162
  differences between people and,
    124–136
  difficult employees and, 115–124
  harassment claims and, 137–152
reluctant witness to sexual harass-
    ment, 149–152
reorganized companies, 190
resolution of differences, 7
  building relationships with em-
    ployees and, 156–157
  coaching employees and, 93–94,
    97–98, 104–105, 108
  competitive peers and, 159
  corrective feedback and, 43
  disagreeing with the boss and,
    12–13
  formal appraisal and, 87–89
  inexperienced workers and,
    72–73
  informal appraisal and, 83
  interviewing prospective em-
    ployees and, 59
  judgmental behavior and,
    127–128
  oral warning and, 171
  shy employees and, 122
resumes, analyzing, 51
rules
  communicating, 178–180
  corrective action and enforce-
    ment of, 182–185
  counseling for violating, 180–182
  firing employees for violating,
    185–187

scripts, value of, 1–2
second interview for prospective
    employees, 56–59, 62–65

sexual harassment
  alleged harasser, talking to,
    145–148
  angry women and, 139–144
  confronting a man about,
    133–136
  reluctant witness to, 149–152
*Sexual Harassment in the Workplace:
  How to Prevent, Investigate, and
  Resolve Problems in Your Organization* (Wagner), 137
shy employees
  communicating with, 120–123
  interview process and, 50–53
sifting through solutions when
    problem solving, 28–30
silence
  breaking barrier of, 121
  pregnant, 4, 37
skill training and hiring decisions,
    50
subjective appraisal language, 79
supervisory positions, hiring for,
    60–65
suppressed problems, 35
surly employees, 85–89
survivors of downsizing, 195–198

tentative plans when problem solv-
    ing, 30–31

uncooperative employees, 25–34

The Wall Street Journal, 190
work history and hiring decisions,
    49, 60
written warnings
  for disciplinary reasons, 184–185
  to improve job performance,
    171–175

You-statements, 18